"The Guideposts outline the new paradigm — the values we must embrace to remain successful on this planet. *Planning for Seven Generations* challenges us to create the future around a vision of what is possible."

Leone Pippard
Canadian Ecology Advocates

"*Planning for Seven Generations* introduces a new way of thinking about our environment, and a new direction for humanity, its message is aimed at the role of each and every individual and at prevailing attitudes in society as a whole."

Geralyne Dionne
Resource Center Librarian, Ecological Agriculture Projects

"A work of great transformational power."

Jo Davis
from notes accompanying the W.C. Good writing award

"If the environmental revolution of the 90's is to succeed, there must be an educational revolution to support it. *Guideposts* should be on the front line of this educational revolution"

EarthKeeper Magazine

"The ideas in *Planning for Seven Generations* are more relevant than ever as we face the task of shifting our collective values — and soon — in a direction consistent with a sustainable life-balance. This work is URGENT and IMPORTANT."

Gordon Ball
Director Program Development, YMCA Geneva Park

First published in 1993
Editor: Elizabeth Jefferson
82 Frontenac Street, Hull, Quebec J8X 1Z5
(819) 778-2946

Guideposts for a Sustainable Future
P.O. Box 374
Merrickville, Ontario, Canada, K0G 1N0

First Edition August, 1993

(The author self-published a limited earlier version with th
same title in 1990: ISBN 0-9694228-0-6)

Canadian Cataloging in Publication Data
Nickerson, Mike, 1951
    Planning for seven generations:
        guideposts for a sustainable future.
ISBN 0-921842-27-9
1. Human ecology. 2. Environmental protection — Citize
participation. 3. Conservation of natural resources —
Citizen participation. I.. Title.
TD170.N44 1993 333.72 C93-090506-7

Printed in Canada.

PLANNING FOR SEVEN GENERATIONS

Guideposts for a Sustainable Future

By Mike Nickerson

Voyageur Publishing

82 Frontenac Street, Hull, Quebec J8X 1Z5 (819) 778-2946

Acknowledgments

This book would not have been possible without help from the following people and organizations.

Editorial suggestions came from Eve Edmonds, Wendy Zatylny, Sean Fordyce, Steven Rowatt, Dr. Gray Merriam, Les Voakes, Seymour Trieger, Doug Crawford, Dan Sullivan, Elizabeth Jefferson and George Mully. The illustrations are the work of John Daveikis, Graham Thomas, Steve Aitken, Simon Hamond and John Bianci.

Contributions for project development and production of this book have come from many sources including the Ontario Ministry of the Environment, the Green Party of Ontario, and the Green Party of Canada, the Helen McCrea Peacock Foundation, the Ottawa Board of Education, Carleton University, the Carleton Board of Education, Canada Trust: Friends of the Environment Foundation, Queen's University, Energy Educators of Ontario. The Harmony Foundation of Canada has also contributed substantially to the printing of this book.

Other contributions and considerable moral support have came form Betty Nickerson, Dr. Mark Nickerson, Ann Mully, George Mully, Dr. Peter Bevan-Baker, David Laine, Howard Gerome, Steve Nickerson, Eric Joss, Susan Noakes, Diane Becket, Peter Padbury, Ralph Torrie, Judy Smith, Burt Harwood, Cam Leslie, Arthur Petch, Rita Burtch, David Faed, Jan Slakov, Gordon Ball, Bev Kettle, Lucy Segatti, Bill Hulett, Ole Hendricson, Orland Gingrich, Peter Au, Brian Rich, and Gerald Pfaff.

Many thanks to all of you and to any others whose names I have missed.

To: Lorna, Lise, Ileana and Julia
and Philippa.

Guideposts

For A Sustainable Future

Activities are sustainable when they:

1. use materials in continuous cycles,

2. use continuously reliable sources of energy,

3. come mainly from the potential of being human (i.e. creativity, communication, coordination, appreciation, and spiritual and intellectual development.)

Activities are not sustainable when they:

4. require continual inputs of non-renewable resources,

5. use renewable resources faster than their rate of renewal,

6. cause cumulative degradation of the environment,

7. require resources in quantities that could never be available for people everywhere,

8. lead to the extinction of other life forms.

Contents

Introduction   **9**

Chapter One:
  The Challenge of Sustainability   **12**

Chapter Two:
  The Environmental Crisis; What We Can Do   **15**

Chapter Three:
  People and the Earth; Our Changing Relationship **24**

Chapter Four:
  Environmental Issues; A Pattern to Remember   **66**

Chapter Five:
  What You Can Do for the Environment   **70**

Chapter Six:
  Our Common Future   **79**

Chapter Seven:
  Working Together for Sustainability   **84**

Chapter Eight:
  Bioregionalism   **91**

Chapter Nine
  Reasons for Hope   **94**

Chapter Ten:
  History of the "Guideposts"   **102**

Chapter Eleven:
  Environmental Problems   **107**

Epilogue: Transformation   **139**

"If we don't change direction, we'll end up where we're going."

author unknown

Introduction

Human kind is coming of age. Since our species was born we have been growing with little worry beyond our immediate needs. Mother Earth always cleaned up after us and provided new frontiers when we outgrew the old.

All this is changing as we reach maturity – as we reach the limits of the Earth's ability to provide for us. With the power and knowledge of maturity comes responsibility. Ours is the classic struggle of adolescence: part of us wants to avoid responsibility and part looks with excitement and anticipation at the challenges and opportunities of adult life.

All around we see consequences of the careless use of adult strength: disappearing fish, oil spills, polluted water, bad air and a sun that burns. It is critical, as a society, that we accept full responsibility for our impact on the environment. The longer we put it off, the harder it will be to regain a healthy relationship with the Earth. If we wait too long it will be too late. It is time for environmental sustainability to be a high-priority component of social and economic policy, as well as individual choice.

Any action starts with an image within a person's mind. The egg you may want for breakfast won't make it to the table until you have imagined it fried, boiled or scrambled. Only with this image in mind can you begin.

Historically, we've never been called upon to imagine the global implications of our actions. Now, we are compelled to do so. Our future – our children's future is being determined now by our ability to bear the global picture in mind and our willingness to act from the concern presented by that picture.

Where are the lines between sustainable and non-sustainable behavior?

What will civilization be like over the centuries to come?

What else can we do if our goal is not just to get bigger?

Planning for Seven Generations is a collection of ideas and information assembled to clarify the issue of sustainability and the possibilities it offers. The Guideposts for a Sustainable Future listed on page 6 provide a checklist for identifying the problems and opportunities of environmentally safe living. They can be used to assess individual plans and actions or institutional policies and development proposals.

This book will clarify these points making it easier to recognize what helps and what hurts the Earth and to see how your life might fit into a sustainable world order. When enough people understand what sustainability means, we can press the issue onto the public agenda. From there, open discussion and common sense will clarify the options and make it possible to adapt on a society wide basis.

People are tremendously clever. We have an extensive collection of information about what we need and what the Earth has to offer and we have the capacity to intricately examine anything else that comes to our attention. We know the problems and most of the solutions. Human beings make all the decisions that effect our relationship with the Earth and our hands direct all the work.

Finding a permanent role for people on the Earth is well within our abilities. The work at hand is to picture the goal, establish it as a clear priority and focus our collective will on bringing it about.

1

The Challenge of Sustainability

There is a tradition within some societies, whenever decisions are being made, to consider the interests of the next seven generations. For the modern world to do the same would mark our passage to maturity.

More than seven thousand generations have cared and toiled to make our lives possible. They have given us language, clothing, music, tools, agriculture, sport, science and a vast understanding of the world within and around us. Surely we are obliged to find ways to allow for at least another seven generations.

It is simply impossible to depend on non-sustainable ways for that long. If civilization is to exist seven generations from now, much will have changed. Forests will have been restored to moderate the land and life. Soils will be used without reducing their fertility. We will have learned to distinguish between basic human needs and luxuries. People will no longer be driven by poverty to abuse their local environments. Extensive use of petroleum will be a thing of the past. The human population will have stopped growing. Mega-armaments will have been abandoned, and security will be seen as a challenge for mutual aid and cooperation. We will likely find as we recognize the limits of physical expansion, that we will again look to the riches of family, community, creativity, compassion, wisdom, wonder and celebration to define the value of ourselves and the status of our societies.

It is a vision beyond the scope of any one person, but as a civilization we see it more clearly each time any one of us pictures one part or another. Vision and the will to survive can generate a sustainable future.

Picture a world in which we know that our childrens' children can securely raise children of their own. Once we have an image of where we must go, getting there becomes much easier. This book looks at the relationship between people and the Earth, how that relationship has changed and the guidelines within which a new stability can be found. Coupled with your understanding of the part of the world in your hands, it will help you visualize a satisfactory and sustainable way to live. When enough people share the vision of a sustainable future, individual efforts will be joined by the vast creativity of our populations and the enormous strength of our institutions. Soon, we could again look hopefully to the future.

An earlier version of *Planning for Seven Generations* was accompanied by a video, "Guideposts for a Sustainable Future." If you feel a visual presentation would be useful for sharing your feelings about sustainability with family, friends and acquaintances, ordering information can be found at the back of the book.

While developing the video and book kit a simple truth was pointed out to me. People pay much closer attention to and learn more from things which they know are relevant to their own lives.

To establish the relevance of sustainability to your life or to the lives of a group preparing to consider the option, ask yourself or the people you are with:

1. What comes to mind when you think about the relationship between yourself and the environment?

2. What concerns do you have about the way people live on this planet?

3. Why are we hearing so much about environmental problems now, when they were hardly known thirty years ago?

4. Where is the effort going to come from to solve environmental problems?

Take a few moments to refresh your personal memories, thoughts and feelings as they are stimulated by each of these questions.

This approach is most effective if you can share what comes to mind with someone else or with several other people. Not only do the responses of others further stimulate one's own thoughts, sharing these thoughts generates the courage to look confidently at the challenges facing us. Try bringing these questions up the next time you are in a conversation and a new topic is in order.

Your thoughts in response to these questions will provide a foundation for your understanding of the basic nature of our changing relationship with the Earth and the challenge of becoming environmentally sustainable.

2

The Environmental Crisis
What We Can Do

For an organism or society to be sustainable, it must provide for its needs in ways that do not destroy its ability to survive.

Sustainability has been the bottom line of evolutionary judgment since life began, but it has taken the considerable problems caused by our rapid growth in population and technical strength for us to realize that sustainability will also be the final measure of human success.

With the publication of *Our Common Future*, the report of the United Nations' World Commission on Environment and Development, authorities confirmed the perils of our non-sustainable ways and the need to restore and preserve the environment. In the commission's words, we have to find ways to:

"... meet the needs of the present without compromising the ability of future generations to meet their own needs."

The challenge is ours.

Where do we start?

15

To start with, we must *not* feel guilty. To blame ourselves or our ancestors would distract from the critical work before us. We have inherited our ways of living from a society to whom the Earth's resources seemed limitless. Practically everything we do was developed without considering sustainability. So it should be no surprise that much of our activities need modification. Some changes can only be made individually, others require that we work together in our communities. The largest of the problems require political action at regional, national and international levels.

What We Can Do.

1. Acknowledge that the problems are critical to our lives.

This book presents an overview of the challenges we face if our society is to sustain itself. After reading it, you can determine if the challenges apply to you.

If you agree we need to develop sustainable ways to live, you have joined a large and growing number of people who feel the same way. Awareness of this expanding agreement will provide the encouragement we need to take on the challenge of planning for seven generations. Making the extent of this agreement obvious is a primary purpose of clearly identifying sustainability as a goal.

2. Learn about the nature of the challenge.

This book outlines the changing relationship between people and the Earth and provides glimpses of what a sustainable world might look like. The Guideposts for a Sustainable Future provide a basic reference for examining the world around us. The material that follows will help you recognize symptoms of the problems, understand their causes and appreciate solutions when you encounter them.

3. Make choices in our own actions.

In the last couple years numerous publications have come out listing actions you can take to reduce your impact on the environment and to help it heal. TV, radio and other media also produce materials for people who want to help. Add to this consumer products being promoted as environmentally friendly and there is much to choose from.

Rather than reproducing these efforts, this book concentrates on developing the ability to independently recognize what helps the Earth to heal and what contributes to the problems. Some of the things we are told will help do not actually do so. When one develops the ability to recognize environmental implications, one can assess development plans and public policy as well as recommended products and activities. After a little practice, one can apply the criteria to one's own short and long-term goals and even contribute to the development of regional, national and international policy on where society is going.

Everyone has a unique background. When we start to apply the design criteria of sustainability to the world as we see it, any one of us could come up with new insights and ideas that can serve us all.

4. Coordinate our efforts.

The likelihood of achieving the goal of sustainability increases with each individual who concludes that it is necessary. Talk with people you know. Express your concerns, and see if others share your views. If the environmental crisis were generally understood and people publicly expressed their feelings about sustainability, social and democratic processes would quickly cause a new social priority to emerge. The efforts of concerned individuals would be greatly amplified by the whole-hearted cooperation of governments and other institutions.

A variety of materials for helping others recognize the challenge of sustainability are listed at the back of the book.

Two major trends, the decline of environmental health and the increase of popular awareness, will lead to resolute action on sustainability.

It is inevitable that these will lead to the motivation necessary for action, but when? Does it come about because we understand the need, or will it take a major environmental collapse to get the point across?

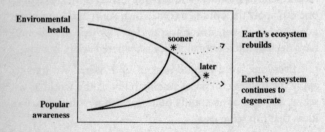

Clearly, it is in our interest to establish the social priority as soon as possible. Once the goal is set, we would see action similar in intensity to the Marshal Plan that transformed Japan and Germany from their post-war ruins into contemporary world leaders. The types of work to be done would differ and the scope of activity would be world wide, but the spirit of investing in the future would set people to work building a world free from the threat of environmental calamity. Businesses, government and other institutions would adapt or be adapted to the requirements of sustainability. Personal efforts would reinforce institutional changes and institutional changes will make it easier to live sustainably.

A Directory of Information on Sustainability

As recognition grows that sustainability is a goal we must achieve, details about reaching the goal become important. There is a great deal of information available, but it is not always found easily when needed.

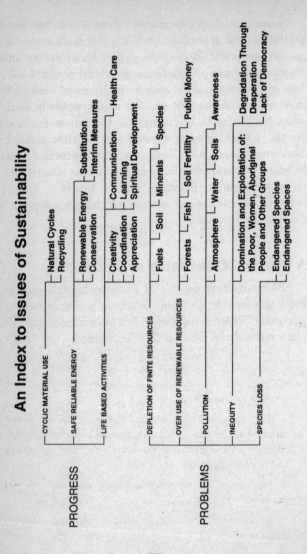

An Index to Issues of Sustainability

PROGRESS

CYCLIC MATERIAL USE
- Natural Cycles
- Recycling

SAFE RELIABLE ENERGY
- Renewable Energy
- Conservation
- Substitution
  - Interim Measures

LIFE BASED ACTIVITIES
- Creativity
- Coordination
- Appreciation
  - Communication
  - Learning
  - Spiritual Development
  - Health Care

PROBLEMS

DEPLETION OF FINITE RESOURCES
- Fuels
- Soil
- Minerals
- Species

OVER USE OF RENEWABLE RESOURCES
- Forests
- Fish
- Soil Fertility
- Public Money

POLLUTION
- Atmosphere
- Water
- Soils
- Awareness

INEQUITY
- Domination and Exploitation of: the Poor, Women, Aboriginal People and Other Groups
  - Degradation Through Desperation
  - Lack of Democracy

SPECIES LOSS
- Endangered Species
- Endangered Spaces

Parallel with the production of this book is an initiative to establish an electronically accessible collection of information on sustainability. The objective of the service would be to collect and organize all the information available on the many problems and opportunities of sustainability. Using electronic storage, retrieval and communication technology this collection of information could be continuously updated and made available through any school or library, or directly over your telephone lines if you have a computer and modem.

The chart here could provide an opening index for finding what you want to know. It can be branched out and developed to include any details related to the problems and solutions of sustainability and to the debate on where humankind is heading and where we want to end up.

Areas of interest covered by the directory would include:

1. Lists of specific actions individuals can take to help ease pressure on the environment, including explanations of how the action helps.

2. Lists of individuals and organizations concerned with the need for sustainability, their areas of interest and where they can be found.

3. Explanations of the issues. Basic statements about environmental issues, including background explanations, different views taken in debates and references to studies and research findings.

4. References to relevant literature and audio-visual materials with abstracts.

5. A collection of visions of what a sustainable future might be like.

21

Debate

There are numerous points which need to be resolved before we can act decisively as a society to meet the environmental challenge. A major function of the *Directory of Information on Sustainability* would be to provide a structure for debate. Any entries could include divergent points of view.

The service would draw attention to points under contention, so they could be easily accessed by anyone wishing to add their experience to resolving the differences.

A nineteenth century philosopher once said

"It is only through the clash of differing opinions that the clear light of truth can shine."

Much truth could be revealed and many smoke screens dissipated by providing a public reference for collecting all the relevant points of view and providing a forum for public discussion.

Further information is available on request.

In *Our Common Future*, the World Commission said:

"... the changes in human attitude we call for depend on a vast campaign of education, debate and public participation."

Through the processes described here we aim to:

1. Promote understanding of sustainability.

2. Clarify the scope of the goal.

3. Help individuals make appropriate decisions in their personal lives and accomplish the goals they set.

4. Resolve differences which retard decisive action.

5. Mobilize the political will needed for institutional adaptation.

Take another look at the Guideposts on page 6. Do they make sense to you?

If you feel they do, we are one step closer to solving the crisis of our non-sustainability.

3

People and The Earth: Our Changing Relationship

Setting the stage for life on Earth

In the vast reaches of space our blue green planet circles around its star — the sun's energy animates the land and moves the water and the air. For billions of years this process has supported life.

Elementary life forms have prepared the way for us; for eons they've eaten away at the bare rock building up the masses of nutrients needed to maintain more complex forms of life.

Daily and seasonal cycles of heating and cooling helped to break up rocks. Countless rainfalls washed exposed surfaces. Simple forms of life found ways to draw out nutrients and synthesize additional materials which they needed for their living forms. As the process continued, loose material accumulated and various organisms found safe habitat in it. The more organisms that lived and died in the developing soils, the more nutrients there were for plants to feed on. With growing reserves of soil and abundant plant life growing from it, the stage was set for animals, first smaller then larger more complex beings. Practically everything taken from the soil by plants and animals returned to it. The soils became richer and more abundant.

All the nutrient elements readily available for use by living things, along with all the material currently caught up in their physical forms is known as the "biomass." "Biological capital" is the biomass plus the profusion of different ways in which life assembles itself. This is the genetic resource of species.

Van Helmont's experiment

The life process has long been a matter of interest and study for curious minds.

At the dawn of our scientific age, a Dutch biologist, Jean Baptist Van Helmont conducted an experiment. In 1652 he wrote:

"I took an earthen vessel in which I put 200 pounds of soil dried in an oven, then I moistened it and pressed into it a shoot of willow weighing five pounds.

After exactly five years the tree that had grown weighed 169 pounds and about three ounces, but the vessel had never received anything but rain water or distilled water

... in the end I dried the soil once more, weighed it and got the same 200 pounds I started with, less about two ounces."

This experiment provides hope for today, because it showed that most of the substance that made up the willow tree's mass, 169 pounds, came from air and water only, air and water that can be found practically every place on Earth. It means that if what we want from the Earth is a good, healthy life for ourselves and our children, the basic demands we make on the planet are minimal.

The basics of human security need not detract from the health of the living Earth. Food, clothing, shelter, health care, companionship and challenge can all be provided for, within and from the natural cycles of the Earth's substance.

Through our imagination and creativity, however, we have found much else to desire. Some of it can be maintained within the Earth's cycles, some of it can not. If being alive, healthy and secure is not satisfying in itself, satisfaction will always be illusive, and there will be no end to the list of things we want. Feeding such endless desires can easily detract from the ability of others to provide for their own basic needs.

26

In the wealthy parts of the world, amidst the endless array of brightly packaged consumer goods, we often fail to appreciate the role of natural ecological systems and resources in sustaining our lives. Yet our survival is dependent on a global balance between what the Earth needs to maintain ecological health and the demands we make on it.

Our spirits and our ability to create are thoroughly enmeshed in the stuff of the Earth.

Our thoughts feelings and imagination have no boundaries. But does our body have a boundary? Most of us would say it does — our skin. However if we consider all the things that cross that boundary in both directions, we would see ourselves in a different light.

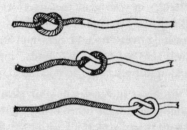

In the illustration above, the rope passes continuously into the knot at one end, and out the other. Before long, the material that originally makes up the knot is entirely replaced by new material, yet the basic pattern of the knot does not change. It is the same with our bodies. Bodily materials change completely every seven years, most of them within a single year, but the basic pattern of our bodies, and of ourselves, remains the same. Most of the substances our bodies will be made of, over the courses of our lives, is outside of our skins right now. All that we have been and all that we will be, is in the soil, water and air about us, our environment. Thus we are literally dumping on ourselves when we release toxins into the environment. On the same basis, if we love ourselves we need also to love the environment, which contains the stuff of our transforming physical forms.

Cycles of Water, Carbon Dioxide and Oxygen

The water present on Earth today is, for the most part, the same water that was here when the planet first cooled.

Water which makes up most of our body continuously cycles all over the earth. Every time you drink something, there are molecules in your glass that have been to every part of the globe. They've come from oceans, lakes, quiet swamps and rushing rivers; from glaciers, rain forests, frost, fog and dew. They've been in clouds, high in the atmosphere and in vast reservoirs deep in the Earth.

Most of the water molecules in your glass have also been in and out of countless other living things. In fact, you may well have shared your drink with every form of life that's ever lived on Earth.

Green plants too are an essential part of ourselves. In a complex series of reactions, plants capture the energy of the sun in the bonds that combine carbon atoms into the molecular chains of simple sugars and starches. These sugars and starches then provide all the energy that the plants use as they grow. They are also the source of all the energy needed by animals that eat plants and, in turn, by animals that eat other animals. Even the lives of bacteria and fungi are ultimately dependent on the work of green plants. These decomposers are powered by releasing small quantities of energy still caught up in dead tissues of the things they consume.

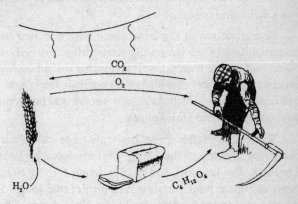

$$6CO_2 + 6H_2O + energy \longleftrightarrow C_6H_{12}O_6 + 6O_2$$

To release the energy bonding the carbon chains together, living things have to take in oxygen. The oxygen helps disassemble the carbon compounds. Carbon dioxide is formed in the process and energy is released. The energy provides life force, and the carbon-dioxide returns to the atmosphere, where it can again be used by plants as they capture the power of the sun.

Through the cycles of carbon, oxygen, water and other materials, the substances that nourish all living things are shared.

Gaia, the living Earth.

The flow of material substance between organisms binds them together in much the same way that the cells of our organs and limbs are bound together by the flow of our blood. From this perspective, all life on Earth can be seen as one single living organism.

Recent studies of the atmosphere have enriched our understanding of the fascinating relationship between our planet and the life it supports. It seems that the atmosphere acts like the feathers of a bird or an animal's fur in that it makes adjustments which maintain a suitable and protective environment for the life it enfolds.

The Gaia hypothesis, as it has come to be called, after the Greek Goddess of the Earth, was formulated by James Lovelock. Dr. Lovelock had been working for the North American Space Administration on a project that sought to develop equipment for detecting life on other planets. They did this by studying the Earth to find signs of life that could be sensed from a distance. The atmosphere, under this investigation, revealed some interesting behavior. The physical nature of the gases found in the atmosphere has been extensively tested. Their behavior in various combinations can thus be predicted by the rules of steady state chemistry. In studying the Earth's atmosphere, however, scientists discovered that it extensively violates the laws of chemistry. The predicted behavior of the gases in the atmosphere should make our planet too hot for any but the most primitive of life forms.

Closer investigations have indicated that the gases of the atmosphere are only a part of the global eco-system. Apparently the rock of the Earth's crust, the oceans, the atmosphere and the life forms they encompass have evolved as a single, tightly-integrated system. The system compensates for changes in the global climate by adjusting the rates at which gases such as oxygen, methane and carbon-dioxide are produced and removed from the atmosphere. This effectively maintains the Earth's climate within the bounds favorable to life as a whole. The observation of this "self-management" has led to the Gaia hypothesis — the hypothesis that the Earth *actively* maintains conditions suitable for the growth and well-being of living things.

Could it be that all the interconnected life forms on Earth, along with the air, water and soil, have some form of collective life beyond that of the "independent" organisms? For some of us, viewing the Earth as a single living organism is a retrieval of ancient wisdom. But for others it's a new concept with the power to change the way we treat the planet and ourselves.

More detail is available in *The Gaia Hypothesis*, by James Lovelock.

Long standing chemical stability leaves us unprepared for the new chemicals that we make and introduce to the environment.

In the beginning, the Earth was a mass of elemental substances. When life started to build its physical forms, it found much of what it needed already present, and what it didn't find, it learned to make.

Life forms have a greater capacity to synthesize compounds than they actually use. Enough different

31

metabolic tricks are in the repertoire to enable any sort of development that life is inclined to. With few exceptions, the number of chemical substances present on the planet came to a stable state a billion years ago. The substances living things had to deal with were the same for countless generations and effective ways were developed to deal with them when they arrived in places where they were not supposed to be.

Today, however, human beings create thousands of new substances every year that have never before been present on Earth. Some are of no consequence and some present serious problems. Because of the continuous cycling that takes place all over the globe, anything we produce, unless handled with extreme care, will eventually confront life of all sorts. Some products of human creation, like pesticides and ozone-depleting substances, have already caused much harm. It is important that we become responsible with our creative abilities and limit irreversible damage.

To find the consequences of your lifestyle, start by multiplying what you do by 5.5 billion.

Each one of us does very little to harm the environment, but very little multiplied by very many is very much. By the same token, when large numbers of people take positive action, enormous problems can be reversed.

The Collective Human Organism

In the study of ecology, there is a field that deals particularly with populations of organisms. A flock of birds for example, will have behavior patterns that are significant and beyond anything that individuals of the species might exhibit. One wolf eating rabbits would have little effect on rabbit populations or the things that rabbits eat and do. But a population of wolves will effect the very nature of rabbits. It is in the context of populations that balances in ecosystems and impact on the environment are observed.

Considering the human family as a collective organism is even more appropriate because our activities are much more interconnected than those of other organisms. Our interconnected activities are felt by the living world as if they were the actions of one being.

We are found in every inhabitable place on Earth. Millions of acres of our crops mine the nutrients of the soil. We consume whole forests, and mountains. Oil wells are like drinking straws in our mouths.

Viewing the human population as one gigantic whole is helpful as we try to grasp how we little humans can have a significant impact on the life of this enormous planet. It is the size to which humanity as a whole has grown, coupled with the might of the mechanical and chemical technologies we use, that have brought us into confrontation with the natural world.

How big have we grown?

How big can we become?

To answer these questions we need to understand something called exponential growth.

Exponential Growth

Throughout history, we have been a tiny presence on Earth. To a large extent, our images of reality are rooted in customs and traditions which originated when our impact was inconsequential. A look at the accelerating nature of exponential growth helps us to comprehend and eventually feel what our cultural heritage has not prepared us for — that there are limits to what we can do to the Earth.

Exponential growth is the growth of something in size or numbers, in proportion to its increasing size or number. You may have observed in the growth of a plant that the more leaves it has catching sunshine, the faster the rate at which it can grow more leaves. Similarly with human populations, the more people there are, the more babies can be born.

One classic example of exponential growth comes from a legend. The King of Persia offered the inventor of the game of chess anything he wanted as a reward. The reward requested was one grain of wheat for the first square on a chess board, two grains for the second, four for the third, eight, sixteen and so on, doubling for each square.

The King agreed, thinking it a modest request that would cost him little. But . . . the amount of grain for the last square alone would have filled a train of box cars wrapped around the Earth at the equator 25 times.

The King simply didn't understand exponential growth and would have had to give away his entire kingdom!

The reason we are so easily deceived and subsequently astonished by exponential growth is because, at first, the increases seem very small and sustainable. After all, quantities can double hundreds, maybe thousands of times before they become significant. However, at a certain point it takes only a few more doublings for the numbers to become very significant.

Clearly anyone telling you that our growth in material consumption or population can be sustained, is (like the King of Persia) unfamiliar with the nature of exponential growth.

* * *

Notable to exponential growth patterns is the length of time it takes for something to double in quantity. The larger the exponent (the rate by which something is growing), the faster the doubling time.

At a growth rate of:	Doubling time is:
1% per year	72 years
3% per year	24 years
5% per year	15 years
10% per year	7 years

Doubling time can be roughly calculated by dividing 72 by the percentage rate.

In the basic exponential progression of 1, 2, 4, 8, 16, 32, etc., we can see that each successive doubling produces a number that is equal to the sum of all the proceeding numbers less one. This makes the point that the next doubling of our population for example, will involve about as many new mouths to feed as have needed to be fed throughout the entire history of human kind.

Think now of what continuous economic growth means. If the economy grows at 5 percent per year, it will double in 15 years. Even at a 3 percent rate of growth, requiring 24 years to double, most individuals would see the doubling of economic activity. Over that 15 to 24 year period, we would have to conduct as much business as has been conducted between the time of the industrial revolution and today. If that isn't staggering, imagine the production necessary to accomplish the next doubling after that. The environment is reeling at today's levels of production. How will it cope if we continue to follow this basic pattern of development?

Particular caution is necessary in a case where something of limited size is being filled or consumed at an exponential rate, such as the Earth's capacity to support human beings or our use of fossil fuels. Just three doublings before further increase or use becomes impossible, only $1/8$ of the total capacity has been involved. One eighth appears insignificant, but it is followed by $1/4$, $1/2$ and then, all the faith in the world will not make further growth possible.

In the 1986 publication *Human Appropriation of the Products of Photosynthesis*, Vitousek, Erlich, Erlich and Matson calculated that human beings were already using 25 percent of the energy captured by plant life world wide. This figure, they say, rises to 40 percent if we only consider land-based vegetation, which makes up the vast majority of human consumption.

It's hard to believe we've reached such levels of activity. However, the very thing that brought on the industrial revolution makes these levels of activity possible — mechanization. The production of goods is no longer tied directly to the physical capability of people. We can spend our time and resources making tools to take over production and then leave the tools to work, while we go on to make more tools to add to the work already being done. We can even set up machines to make machines to make the goods and so multiply the effects of human effort again and again. Assuming they are maintained, all these machines will run as long as they are provided with energy. And energy reserves, although diminishing, are still vast. Unless there is a change of political will to adopt a goal other than growth, we can and will continue to grow until we overshoot some limitation and collapse.

When the possibility of perpetual growth is so obviously impossible, one might wonder why our established orders stick to it so religiously. Herman E. Daly, a Senior Economist from the Environmental Division of the World Bank, expressed it beautifully:

"The growth ideology is extremely attractive politically because it offers a solution to poverty without requiring the moral disciplines of sharing and population control."

In a rather rough shod fashion this strategy has worked for centuries, accounting for the faith that many modern leaders still put in perpetual growth as a solution to our problems. As increasingly severe social and ecological problems testify however, we are going to have to be more imaginative and possibly even morally responsive, in the future.

A Fundamental change has come about in our relationship with the Earth

Exponential growth in production and population over the last several generations has changed our relationship with the Earth. Considering that less than a century ago human activities were scarcely one percent of what they are today, we can get some idea of why the social and economic institutions which served us well for the last 100 years and more, are not prepared for the new circumstances.

Throughout history the limits of the Earth were seldom considered because they were far beyond our reach. Suddenly, with the last few doublings of our activities, we are encountering those limitations in numerous places. Now it matters what we do and how we do it. How long will it take to evolve our customs and institutions to accommodate this new reality?

For the last thirty years, single decades have seen more growth and more consumption than have previous centuries and even millennia. Today we influence practically everything on Earth, even the life processes on which we depend.

Our tremendous growth has brought relative prosperity and abundance of human life at the expense of the environment. We overuse and deplete our resources; forests, minerals, soil fertility — we're living on environmental capital, by depleting that capital we steal from future generations.

The difference between living on "capital" and living on the "interest derived from capital" makes the analogy of environmental capital useful. The interest on "environmental capital" would be the regenerative capacity of renewable resources or the repeated utility gained from the cyclic use of non-renewable resources. We deplete environmental capital when: we use non-renewable resources in ways that make them unavailable for further use, when we use renewable resources faster than they can regenerate and when we cause the extinction of other species.

Ecology

In 1869, Ernest Haeckel coined the word "Ecology" to represent the study of the relationships between different organisms and between organisms and their surroundings. Studies of these relationships had been going on before then, but they had not been identified as a collective science. Ecology includes the flow of materials between organisms, mutual dependencies and the factors that limit growth. Of particular interest are two categories of limitations:

The first are the *limitations of resource supplies*, caused by the depletion or absence of some nutrient or other material needed to maintain a way of life.

The second are the *limitations of tolerance* — tolerance to climatic differences, tolerance to toxic substances, and tolerance to competition.

These limitations determine why some creatures can live in one place and others can't, why a particular life form is abundant in one location and only occasionally found in another and why they sometimes pass from existence altogether.

Past civilizations unable to accommodate these limitations either succumbed to them or were forced to move elsewhere. For today's global civilization, accommodation is the only answer, moving elsewhere is no longer an option.

Archaeologists investigating the disappearance of a civilization that once thrived on Easter Island suspect a progression of events that contains a lesson for us all. It appears that the Island's population had been growing for some time. When they became over crowded, two factions emerged and warred with each other. The winning faction continued to grow in numbers until they exhausted the island's resources. Having over-taxed their environment's capacity to support them, most of the island's population died out, leaving little but monuments to attest to their former greatness.

41

Economics is three fifths of ecology

Although ecology and economics are both derived from the Greek word "oikos" (meaning living place), it has been said that economics concerns itself with only three fifths of ecology. Economics can be boiled down to the three stages of:

1. assembling materials;

2. production of a product from the materials;

3. the distribution of the product.

To these activities, acknowledged by our accounting systems, ecology adds:

4. the effect on the resource base from which the materials are taken; and

5. the effect which by-products of production and used goods have when they become waste.

These two additional concerns correspond to the categories of limitations outlined above.

The principle of diminishing resources can be easily understood by anyone who has seen a big bottle of peanut butter or jam slowly diminish over the weeks. Eventually there is only enough left for one more sandwich — then it's gone. In spite of the simplicity of this principle, until recently, high-level policy decisions dealing with resource development have not taken it into account.

The limitation of tolerance is well illustrated in the making of wine. Yeast eats the sugars in fruit juices and excretes alcohol as a by-product. When the level of alcohol reaches 14 percent, the yeast can no longer tolerate it and dies. This is why the alcohol content of wine is never more than 14 percent. Drinks with a higher alcohol content have to be refined by people.

The idea that economics is three fifths of ecology and that our lack of consideration for the other two fifths is the root of the environmental crisis is presented in more detail in Chapter 4, *Environmental Issues: A Pattern to Remember*.

War as a means of overcoming limitations

One of the most dangerous responses to resource depletion is the tendency for nations faced with shortages to make war on other nations to supplement their supplies.

Resource control has long been a driving force in armed conflicts. History speaks of innumerable peoples who, having grown to the capacity of their territories, set out to conquer the people and territories around them. Often this would be in order to collect and control resources in the forms of slave labor, riches, land and or taxes.

With the advent of industrialization, the first nations that utilized mechanized production to make weapons had a great advantage over everyone else. They carried on the tradition of empire building and carved up almost the entire planet into colonies to enrich their respective states.

It was easy for colonial empires, with guns and navies, to conquer non-industrialized peoples but the conflicts between industrial powers were major contests. The stakes were high. To defeat another colonial power was to take over established colonies, already organized for the extraction of wealth.

Industrialization itself was developing, and the participating nations were no doubt feeling great surges of strength as their factories found more and more effective ways to produce increasing quantities of guns, ammunition and other instruments of power. The two World Wars can be seen as all-out applications of industrial might, seeking to control the spoils of global empire.

Because the industrial powers were fairly equally matched, the grandest of imperial adventures, the World Wars, led to no particular gains. In fact, the outcome of the Second World War was an international moral condemnation of direct colonial rule. Any further advantage to be taken of other countries had to be maintained in much subtler ways.

The lesson: that colonialism was successful because the colonizers had greater productive strength than their victims, rather than because their race was any better, has been slow to sink in. However, we have seen its repeated proof in the efforts to control Vietnam and Afghanistan. Try as they might, the two most powerful nations on Earth were unable to control much smaller nations who had access to industrially-produced weapons and were familiar with and loved their homelands as well.

The Vietnam War marked the end of an era in which nations could acquire new resources by forcefully maintaining control of other territories. Did anyone notice that the oil crisis first came to public attention within a month of the U.S. withdrawal from Vietnam? The Soviet retreat from Afghanistan simply confirmed the end of traditional colonialism and eliminated the possibility of the lesson being confused by differences in the ideologies promoted by intruding powers.

Of the conflicts taking place today, practically all are contests for control of resources — minerals, land, labor, markets — or the security of supply routes that make resources accessible. These conflicts are frequently instigated by peoples who lost control of their territories in colonial times and are trying to reestablish their rights to them. Such uprisings would be short-lived and successful, if it weren't for generous contributions of money, military training and weapons provided by previous colonial powers in exchange for continued access to these countries' resources.

Showdown in the Middle East

Old habits are hard to change.

There have been some encouraging signs indicating that world powers are starting to realize their security depends less on huge military preparations than on the well-being of their peoples and the environment. However, the amount of weaponry prepared and ready to be used tomorrow amounts to some six thousand times the total of all weapons used during the entire Second World War, including the two atomic bombs used near the wars end. Perhaps the greatest danger of these weapons being used is the potential for a conflict over the diminishing supplies of oil, the greatest reserves of which are located in the Middle East. Already, military preparedness in that territory amounts to 40 percent of the world's $1,000,000,000,000-a-year "defense" spending. Will we be able to make the

45

changes necessary to live without oil before some industrial power attempts to seize control of the last oil reserves? The recent shoot-out in Kuwait and Iraq was largely a cooperative venture among industrial powers against Iraq. Such assertions of control might proceed differently if the spoils were seen as too limited to go around.

If Armageddon is to be fought, it may well be between large non-sustainable economies trying desperately to control disappearing oil supplies.

Control of resource supplies is not the only security issue we face, however. Security institutions could contribute significantly to environmental recovery. Human beings have survived because of our ability to work together to overcome common obstacles. Traditionally, the greatest threat to a nation's security has come from other groups organized to invade and take over. To guard against this, standing armies have long been maintained, through contributions of money and labor from the general population.

In the meantime, a new and greater threat to our security has arisen: environmental disruption. To meet this threat, all sectors of society have to respond, but defense institutions in particular have a responsibility. After all, they are well-paid by tax revenues to guard our security.

Think of what departments of defense could do if they clearly included environmental security in their mandates. The military is accustomed to developing and conducting training courses. They have scientists and engineers familiar with designing specialized equipment and they have hundreds of thousands of people organized and disciplined to take on any tasks they are ordered to. Imagine the

European Community, Japan and the United States engaging in a competition to see whose forces could establish the most extensive tree covers in desert and deforested regions. Military assets could be used effectively to clean up polluted areas, monitor environmental indicators and aid in the reorganization necessary to become sustainable.

Social awakening to environmental problems

The environment has ranked among the top concerns of a majority of the population for many years now. It is no wonder, given the long list of serious environment related issues that have come to public attention.

The rise of popular awareness can be traced back to the publication of Rachel Carson's book, *Silent Spring*, in 1962. Ms. Carson had noted a significant decline in the number of birds where she was living. She traced this occurrence to the application of pesticides that not only poisoned insects, but also the birds that ate the insects. This connection is now widely understood, and in many parts of the world the use of some of the most serious poisons is severely restricted, or banned altogether. However, at the time, the established order discounted the analysis, condemned Ms. Carson for disturbing the public and ostracized her from the scientific community.

Nevertheless, the alarm had been sounded, and other individuals started to look into the effects of human activities on the life of the Earth. More books and articles were written, and more people became concerned. Add to this the increase in people directly affected by one problem or another: increases in respiratory ailments, rates of cancer, and serious allergy problems; mass evacuations due to industrial accidents, climatic change, disappearing wilderness and a host of other indicators. All of these have attuned people to the enormous threat environmental imbalance poses to our collective security.

As the 1990s progress, popular sentiment is approaching critical mass — the point where a clear majority of people can demand that sustainability become the mandate of our social institutions.

Governments recognize this concern enough to pay extensive lip service to it. However, as long as only a tiny portion of our tax money is being used to address environmental problems, compared to the billions of dollars that are being funneled into military spending and industrial expansion, we have to be wary of our governments' sincerity and make every effort to convince them that they must respond to our concerns. If they do not, we must replace them with people who will.

Environmental problems are economic, political and social.

In the *economic* sphere, there is danger arising from different ways of assessing value. Take a forest, for example. Through a straight-forward investment in labour and equipment, a forest can be clear cut and turned directly into a large amount of money. The value of the forest is less clear in terms of its role in stabilizing soils, absorbing carbon-dioxide and providing habitat for other creatures. Along with recreational uses and even the sale price of forest products selectively removed for generations to come, this sustainable value is many times greater than the value of cashing in the whole forest with one cutting. In this broader context, the forest's worth is divided between the businesses using the forest over the next seven (or seventy) generations, and the money that doesn't have to be spent from the public purse in order to clear up silted water ways, combat global warming and revive the species diversity that make for a healthy ecosystem. In the long run the forest is worth far more when managed sustainably, but the company that clear cuts has the money in hand and can use that money now to promote its goals and interests.

The economic system is clearly stacked in favor of short term gain. Significant counter-balances have to be agreed upon and implemented if market forces are to be part of the solution to the environmental crisis.

The *political* sphere, which is the most likely source of economic discipline, is unfortunately very responsive to money and, by association, to the forces that turn environment into wealth. Governments need money to provide services for all of us, and the individuals that make up governments also need money in order to get re-elected.

The *social* sphere is where the buck stops. Only a clear majority demand will surpass the influence of money and produce a society committed to sustainability. Our governing bodies must institute programs with this goal in mind and with enough incentives and deterrents to make it in the interest of businesses to accommodate the same ends. With the institutions addressed, we must also realize what aspects of our lifestyles add to the problems and where they add to the solutions. What we know in our minds must effectively make its way to the action center of our hearts. We must develop a strong love for our planet, for future generations and for ourselves so that we enthusiastically choose sustainable ways, rather than choosing what the persuasive forces of consumer culture tell us we should want.

Before the Second World War, Rudolf Steiner expressed concern that all the power and resources of society were concentrating in the hands of the economic sector. He saw the rise of industrial militarism as a serious consequence of this trend. As an alternative, he proposed that: *although the economic sector produces the wealth, the use of that wealth should be evenly distributed for allocation between the social, cultural and economic sectors.* The activities and services of government and other social agencies should use their portion in accordance with their mandate. Similarly, the cultural sector should promote values, the arts and entertainment for the well-being and enrichment of society, according to the criteria of the people involved. Of course, the economic sector would continue to direct its affairs in its own interests.

Steiner's work received insufficient attention to deter the power concentrations that led to World War Two. We may consider reviving the ideas in his book, *Towards Social Renewal*, as we seek balance in society today.

Our Common Future

On April 27, 1987, the World Commission on Environment and Development (WCED) — also known as the Brundtland Commission — presented its report, *Our*

Common Future, to the United Nations. Their observation, after a three-year, world-wide investigation into the relationship between the environment and human development practices was that:

> **"Many present efforts to guard and maintain human progress, to meet human needs, and to realize human ambitions are simply unsustainable — in both the rich and poor nations. They draw too heavily, too quickly, on already overdrawn environmental resource accounts to be affordable far into the future without bankrupting those accounts."**

Their message was not a message of doom. Rather, it was an *"urgent notice"* that we must take these matters seriously and correct the situation. They are hopeful that it is indeed within our ability to avoid disaster, providing we get on with the task.

It had been said before, but never with such authority. The members of the Commission were highly experienced and respected representatives from 21 nations. They carried out their investigation in such a comprehensive manner that conventional wisdom now recognizes we are facing a crisis. Before the report became public, as any long-standing environmentalists will testify, calls for action were easily dismissed or ignored. Since the report, this is no longer the case.

There is more on the Brundtland Commission and its report in Chapter 6.

Sustainable Development

The Brundtland Commission advises that the solution to our pressing crisis is sustainable development. Sustainable development they define as *"development that meets the needs of the present without compromising the ability of future generations to meet their own needs."* It is interesting to compare this with the Native American notion that making decisions must take into account the needs of the next seven generations. In further explanation the Commission states:

At minimum, sustainable development must not endanger the natural systems that support life on Earth: the atmosphere, the waters, the soils, and the living beings.

The Guideposts for a Sustainable Future

Does any doubt remain that our relationship to the environment is the most pressing issue of our times?

If you agree that heedless development is a threat to the future, there are guidelines to help us identify the activities we must ease up on, those we must stop and the areas with abundant opportunities for sustainable growth.

This book revolves around the principles known as the Guideposts for a Sustainable Future. They are called Guideposts because they indicate directions. They are design criteria for finding sustainable ways to live.

Sustainability can be defined as the ability to stay alive over the long run. For human kind, this means a period of time longer than any individuals can expect to live, for seven generations, a thousand years, or perhaps until the sun expires.

Activities which are sustainable:

1 Use materials in continuous cycles.

Pictures from space show our blue and green planet as a small sphere orbiting with its moon in a vast emptiness. A closer look reveals that the layer of materials actually of use to living things on the Earth is only a very thin film over the planet's surface.

Within this limited stock of materials, any substances needed regularly must, over time, be used again and again. The cycles which bring the needed materials back for reuse must either occur naturally, like the cycles of water and carbon, or they must be maintained through mindful recycling programs.

2 Use continuously reliable sources of energy.

As vast as current supplies of coal and oil are, we are consuming them far more quickly than they are created. The dangers of releasing all the carbon in these resources aside, their massive use cannot be our custom if civilization is to be a permanent presence on Earth. The same is true of energy from nuclear fission. The troubles of enormous cost and danger may be overcome, but the raw fuel is also limited in supply.

Usable power from nuclear fusion, which has practically unlimited fuel, is only theoretical at this point. Should it be harnessed, extensive testing would be necessary before claims of safety and reliability could be established and dependency on it considered.

This leaves heat from the Earth's core, the sun (actually nuclear fusion at a safe distance) and the wind and the water which the sun sets into motion. These power sources are abundant, and can be harnessed practically anywhere. With the exception of the problems associated with large dams, renewable sources of energy have little or no negative environmental impact.

3 Come mainly from the potentials of being human.

Once we have secured the food and shelter necessary for healthy life, worlds of opportunity open up for personal growth and satisfaction. The 3 L's — learning, love and laughter — as well as friendship, art, music, dance, sport, communication, service and appreciation of the universe within and around ourselves, can all make life worthwhile. They can provide pleasure, purpose and meaning to our lives without harming the Earth

Activities which are not sustainable:

4 Require continual inputs of non-renewable resources.

Non-renewable resources are resources available only in limited quantity. Metals, coal and oil are notable examples. They can be very useful, even essential, for building a sustainable society, but if our way of life always requires that more and more of these materials be extracted, we will eventually run out. Dependency at that point would be disastrous.

5 Use renewable resources faster than their rate of renewal.

Renewable resources are resources which grow and increase through natural processes. Some examples are forests, fish stocks, ground water and soil fertility. As long as the rate at which they are used is not greater than the rate at which they grow or accumulate, the situation can remain viable. When the rate of use exceeds the rate of renewal, the stock will become depleted and problems will follow.

6 Cause cumulative degradation of the environment.

Certain amounts of pollution are cleansed by natural processes. When we create waste which nature cannot handle, or which cannot be absorbed as fast as we create it, the pollution builds up causing problems which become more and more serious as the activity continues.

7 Requires resources in quantities that could never be available for people everywhere.

The cooperation needed to build a sustainable world order will not come about as long as some groups of people take unfair advantage of others. Inequity often leads to social strife and armed conflict. Furthermore, the people at the bottom of the pyramid of exploitation are often forced by desperation to overexploit the environment around them for day to day survival. The degradation of their territories not only makes life worse for them, it undermines the global systems which provide for those at the top of the pyramid as well as those below.

8 Lead to the extinction of other species.

The web of life is intricate and mutually supportive. Many species have passed from existence and the web still holds. However, it is weakened with each life form lost. If we maintain patterns of development which regularly destroy other forms of life, we progressively undermine our own existence as a part of the global ecosystem. With the loss of species we also lose genetic possibilities for fighting disease in people and in food crops, as well as potential new sources of food.

Do you think these eight points are accurate? Or, do you think a sustainable society can exist within other boundaries? It is important to clarify the design criteria if we hope to focus our collective potential.

One possible deficiency has been pointed out in this frame of reference. Some people contend that it will be impossible to achieve sustainability until people affected by a decision have the right to be involved in making that decision. How can the delicate choices necessary to develop a sustainable balance be made without involving the eyes, ears and minds of the people directly involved in a situation? Much of the hope we have for solving today's crisis comes from the enormous potential of the concerned population. This potential is lost if people are not involved in the decisions and the work that shape our world. Essentially we are talking about democracy. Not just the occasional opportunity to have a say in who will wield authoritarian power for the next four or five years, but actual involvement of people in the decision-making of governance.

Opponents of this notion foresee dictatorship by a population with values and beliefs shaped by mass media, which for the most part is controlled by rich commercial interests. Nonetheless, as the information age unfolds and more and more people become able to distribute their thoughts, the possibility of a broadly informed population is quickly rising. Community involvement in decisions effecting the community may yet become another Guidepost.

One-quarter of the World's population consumes three-quarters of the World's goods.

Perhaps the most difficult point for people in affluent countries to accommodate from the Guideposts framework is the notion of living in a way that doesn't impoverish others. Nevertheless, our well-being depends on this. As long as one quarter of the world's population consumes $3/4$ of the world's goods, billions of people in poorer countries will be forced by poverty to over stress their environment in order to supply us and scratch out a living for themselves.

Some of the excessive pressures on the global environment would be alleviated with the end of poverty, but developing nations aspire to do more than just end their desperation. They have been presented with countless expressions of our consumer values by companies eager to sell to the fortunate few who can buy imported goods.

Third world economies are developing. If, by example, we maintain the ethic of growth for growth's sake, in both production and consumption, it will lead to disastrous

57

consequences in terms of competition over resource supplies and a multiplication of the already unacceptable levels of environmental contamination. For the developed world to have any credibility in our efforts to secure the environment, we will have to set an example that promotes equal opportunity for all people.

Not a return to the 1800's

Some people think becoming sustainable means returning to some pre-electric darkness. Not so. We have learned to do a great deal in modern times that improves our lives without stressing the Earth. Now that we have reached the limits of our planet, however, we must be discriminating about what techniques we use. Some technologies and ways of living present mortal dangers, but other modern innovations can give us more healthful, secure and enjoyable lives. Better understanding of nutrition and health care can make our lives longer and stronger. Great strides have been taken in the efficiency and cleanliness of many technologies. The production of durable, easily repaired goods would reduce resource consumption and free up much personal time that would otherwise be spent making, buying and paying for disposable goods. Similarly, the end of population growth will lighten our loads, in that we will only have to maintain housing stocks and other infrastructure, rather than having to double their capacity every 20 years.

Conventional economics needs modification here. Presently, when people have enough and are not buying more, others go without work and meet hard times. Let us remember that the productive capacity of one person has multiplied a hundred fold in the last century or two. Even so, people managed to raise their children to maturity long before that. We have to somehow realize that with our modern ingenuity and productive capacity we can provide for everyone without everyone working all the time. *As long as there are people in need, there will be work to do. When there is no work to do, it will be time to celebrate.* An attitude recognizing this would balance work and leisure and contribute to a sustainable world. However, at this point a great deal of work is necessary to clean up the mess from the last 50 years. There is no shortage of work to be done; it is only a shortage of good will and imagination, among the leaders in our society, which keeps people who want to work away from the tasks at hand.

In his book, *The Frontiers of Being*, Duncan Blewett identifies what he calls the "Law of Feeling." In essence, it says that when we do something for someone else, we tend to feel good about ourselves and consequently about the world. In this context the opportunity to work, to provide for human needs, in a situation where there are not endless volumes of work available, might come to be an indulgence we look forward to.

There have been other developments in the understanding of human character: how to raise children while preserving a maximum of their natural potentials; how to make peace with our personal pasts so as to meet the future with confidence and clarity; and how to relieve stress and see life as something to be enjoyed, rather than just existing to be stimulated by an endless progression of consumer items. Such developments can provide enormous improvements in the quality of human existence. In so doing, they can make it much easier for us to let go of the activities we are coming to realize are destructive to the environment.

We can meet all the requirements for a full healthy life without stretching the planet beyond its limits.

Becoming sustainable is the new definition of progress. To develop non-sustainable projects is to be going backwards.

"Our ignorance is not so vast as our failure to use what we know."
                                                                M.K. Hubbert

"Our only enemy is our unwillingness to adapt our pattern of living to our environment."   Raymond Dasman

By facing ecological reality we learn that some kinds of growth are life-supporting and others are life-threatening. Some doors to development will close as we discover unacceptable dangers.

Other doors, to activities which are sustainable, will remain open.

As the will to become sustainable grows and priorities shift, a whole new range of activities will arrive to provide work.

• There is a tremendous amount of work needed to restore environmental health.

• Durable, useful, easily maintained goods will find greater acceptance.

• In response to the apparent inability of huge operations to sense their impact on the environment and on the lives of the people where they operate, we may see a shift toward a larger number of smaller enterprises that can work more closely with their surroundings and can take advantage of the decentralized nature of renewable energy and nutrient resources.

• There will be an increasing shift to activities based on what we can do with the abilities which life bestows on us.

Global Communications Access

Communications services are a popular example of modern technology that can likely be maintained in a sustainable manner. It has become possible over the last hundred years to provide an ever greater capacity for communications using ever smaller amounts of materials and energy. Already this capacity has caused great changes in our world. The extension of its potential could be as significant to human beings as brains were for the organisms that developed nerve communications between individual cells.

Global communications access would mean that any human being — rich or poor — would have the right to use a network of wires and satellites to communicate with any other human being on the planet. The advantages of such a right are many: small businesses would become more viable, information about world events could be gathered directly, relationships could be developed between people in different countries, and bonds could be maintained between family members and friends wherever they happen to roam. With propaganda subject to anyone's verification, international understanding promoted by direct contact and a strong web of unbroken relationships encircling the globe, communications access could contribute much to a

61

peaceful world. The technology necessary for this to be possible is far less complex than some new weapons systems, and the cost would be only a fraction of what is currently spent on arms.

Life-Based Pursuits

Life-based pursuits are activities based on resources that do not diminish with use. They require little more than our capacities as human beings and include friendship, love, art, music, dance, sport, recreation, looking, listening, smelling, touching, tasting, thinking, meditating, learning and anything else that comes from developing and using the capabilities which being human offers.

These capabilities tend to become stronger and more rewarding through use. Furthermore, one person's participation in one or another of these activities does not diminish anyone else's opportunities. In fact, the better someone gets at a life-based activity, the greater their ability to entertain others and to teach them to grow in a similar manner.

It is interesting, even exciting, to contemplate how our society would be different if life-based pursuits were encouraged instead of the conventional values of accumulation and consumption. With the goals of accumulation and consumption, once someone collects more than their share of materials, someone else will have to do with less. The fact that our neighbour's success may be at our expense or that our nation's prosperity may be at the expense of other nations is likely the cause of much personal and international tension. If on the other hand, once the material necessities of healthy life are ensured, we turned to the development of our human potentials to satisfy the urge to grow, we would likely find different results.

Because life-based development does not depend on vast material resources, it's not likely to inspire organized conflict. Quite the contrary. By developing human potentials we increase our personal satisfaction and simultaneously reduce our territorial and material needs. The more we develop our skills and abilities the more we can help others grow. Sports, music and other creative activities give pleasure to both participants and observers. As we develop our own inner calm, we can help others find calm in their lives. As we increase our understanding we can help others to understand.

It is therefore to our personal advantage to encourage others to excel in these pursuits. The mutual support and assistance that could develop from such a change of focus is what we need now to pool our abilities and meet the challenge of sustainability.

"If only men could see each other as agents of each others' happiness, they could occupy the Earth, their common

habitation, in peace, and move forward confidently together to their common goal.

The prospect changes when they regard each other as obstacles; soon they have no choice left but to flee or be forever fighting. Humankind then seems nothing but a gigantic error of nature."

Abbé Sieyes,
Prelude to the Constitution 1789, France

The prospects for the future improve when we place more value on the quality of life than on the quantity of goods we consume.

From our earliest recollections growth has been a primary concern. Oh, to be able to fetch toys for one's self! To reach the light switch or the water tap! These are commonly held aspirations from the first years of our lives. They leave a lasting impression and there is no sign that our urge to grow ever stops. However, as we reach a certain physical size, we do stop growing in height. A good thing too — if we didn't stop growing, our bodies would soon become unmanageable. As a civilization we must also stop growing physically before we are too big for our planet.

Our growth as individuals doesn't stop with physical maturity, however. In fact, many people find that they had barely started to grow as individuals when the task of attaining physical maturity was completed. The expansion of our understanding, skills, relationships and other products of living, continue throughout our lives. There is no reason to suspect that our society's growth would stop with physical maturity either.

Individually, as our personal satisfaction increases, we find our material needs reduced. As societies focusing on the increased satisfaction of our members, we will likely find that the same is true. Many more people will be able to get much more out of life, and all of us will be able to expect as much for our children.

Do we share the goal of a Sustainable Future?

In the past, enormous tasks have been accomplished when societies identified a common goal. Today we face a challenge as great as any that faced our ancestors. We know the problems and most of the solutions. There's no question about our ability to put things right. After all, human beings make all the decisions and do all the work that affect our relationship with the Earth.

The question is: Can we agree on a common goal?

We live in the strongest, most knowledgeable civilization that has ever existed on this planet. We can accomplish anything possible if it is established as a collective goal.

Do you share the goal of a sustainable future?

Do your friends, families and acquaintances share this goal? By asking through all available channels we may yet focus the resolve necessary to change direction before it is too late.

4

Environmental Issues
A Pattern to Remember

Economics is 3/5 of Ecology:

Resources - MATERIALS - PROCESSING - DISTRIBUTION - Waste

All Environmental problems are the result of overlooking the resource base and waste

---

For all its complexity, the entire range of economic activity can be looked at in terms of three basic steps.

1) Assembly of *materials*:

This can mean locating or gathering raw materials like soil and seed, metallic rocks and energy; or it can be the assembly of information and images.

2) *Processing* the assembled materials:

Planting, cultivation and harvesting; extracting metal from the ore and forming it into useful items; or organizing the information into a coherent, useful or entertaining format.

3) *Distribution* of the end product:

Getting the produce, the goods, or the report, film or whatever has been produced to places where they can be used and appreciated.

In a well-developed economy, the raw material for one economic activity is often the product from one or several other activities. However, these three steps are basic to them all.

From an *ecological* viewpoint, these same three steps are present. Plants and animals collect nutrients, process (digest) them into useful forms and distribute them to organs and limbs for use in their growth and activities. Sometimes creatures even gather materials and form them into "artifacts" for specific purposes; such as nests, honeycombs and beaver dams.

In both the human economy and the natural world, these steps of materials, production and distribution are accompanied by two further considerations: the natural resource base and waste. In economics these concerns have seldom been accounted for. In the study of ecology, however, the limitations these impose are often observed and sometimes explained as the "law of the minimum" and the "law of tolerance."

The law of the minimum states that growth will continue drawing on available resources as needed, until one of them is exhausted. The first to be used up is the limiting factor.

The law of tolerance deals with the ability of different organisms to tolerate changes in their living conditions. Changes in climatic conditions or the chemical composition of their surroundings can lead to intolerable and therefore limiting situations, as can the arrival of a competing organism or a new predator.

These "laws" govern all life on earth. Many organisms are integrated with other life forms in such a way that the "waste" from one is the raw material for another. Such relationships tend to keep resource limitations and waste accumulation from becoming a problem. On the other hand, if an organism does exhaust a necessary resource or if it produces waste materials that change its habitat beyond its ability to adapt, it must migrate or perish. We humans have always been mobile and with our remarkable ability to find different ways of doing things, we have not had to pay much attention to the limitations of our environment. However, now that our population has grown to cover most of the globe, and our mechanical and chemical technologies have reached enormous proportions, we are faced with serious problems which result from approaching either the limitations of the resource base or the limitations of tolerance.

If Mother Nature were to present invoices for resources extracted and wastes absorbed, conventional economic accounting would be able to keep human activities in balance with the rest of the natural world. Nature is suffering from our use and abuse, but she issues no bills. It is up to us to tally the value of the services we take from her and pay the cost. If we honor our debt, we will have the resources needed to correct the problems we've caused and prevent catastrophe.

The problems resulting from our traditional neglect of ecology's other two fifths are listed here in columns indicating which of ecology fifths they are coming from.

Problems of Tolerance

Acid Rain

The Green House Effect

Ozone Depletion

Municipal Waste

Industrial Waste

Nuclear Waste

Water Pollution

Pesticides

Environmental Illness

Problems of Resource Supply

Depletion of Soil Quality

Deforestation

Ground Water Depletion

Non-Renewable Resource Depletion

Energy Depletion

Loss of Habitat

Species Extinction

Poverty

Problems of Both

Destruction of Aboriginal Cultures

Militarism

Over-Population

The problems listed here are briefly explained in Chapter 11.

5

What You Can Do For The Environment

Individual Action:

Most bookstores offer a number of "What You Can Do For the Environment" books dedicated to everyday actions that lighten our impact on the Earth. Rather than reproducing such lists, this chapter looks at some less common approaches.

• What impact can one person have? The will to act is often clouded by doubts about one's ability to influence anything substantially. Personal actions are the root of trends. Think of what you do as a sample of what anyone might do. What would the impact of your actions be if the billions of other people sharing the planet did the same as you? The consequences, whether positive or negative, represent the potential of the attitude.

• Perhaps the biggest impact we can have for a minimum of effort comes from adjusting habits. Habits are like the default settings on a computer. Default settings are the things a computer does automatically unless it is told to do otherwise. If you don't like a particular setting, a little effort can change it, and afterwards it will automatically do what you want. Our habits, like default settings, save us a

70

lot of time because we don't have to think through a routine every time we perform common tasks. However, if a habit is wasteful or polluting, a short period of concentration can change it to one that is more appropriate. Enormous savings can be produced over a lifetime, thanks to such adjustments.

• The 3R's — Reduce, Reuse and Recycle — have proved effective in communicating the essence of waste avoidance. The 'R' that can tune us into resource concerns is 'Respect.' If we respect the life of trees and the ecological service of forests, we will use paper and other wood products recognizing that they have value beyond what we pay for them. If we respect soil fertility as the source of our health and as the bank in which the bodies of future generations are deposited, we would care for its vitality and return whatever we take from it. The same can be said for respecting water, the primary substance in all life and for respecting the energy we take from dwindling reserves or from limited sources. By developing a deep appreciation for the things that make our lives possible, we will be inclined to treat them well.

• So many environmental problems are aggravated by the way modern life tends to separate us from the natural world. The more we get caught up in our own creations — buildings, transportation systems, media, social intrigues —

the less contact we have with the life supporting processes of nature. A first step toward regaining one's connection with the world around us is to get to know the systems that connect society with the Earth. Visit the local water treatment plant and get a feeling for the volumes and processes that it works with. Check out the solid waste facilities. Find out where your electricity and oil come from and where your food is produced. When we use these services, we are by extension at the site carrying out whatever process takes place there. Any understanding of, or experience with, these processes will increase our comprehension of how we interact with the environment.

• Developing a direct relationship with the natural world can multiply our effectiveness in understanding and addressing environmental problems.

• Spending time in natural settings helps to develop one's appreciation of them.

• Planting seeds and taking care of the plants that grow can also help you to "tune in." A yearly ritual of planting seeds, nurturing the plants to maturity and saving their seeds to plant the following year encompasses the whole life cycle and can lead to insights that are beyond words.

• Planting young trees, caring for them in their first years and watching them grow over the years that follow can further develop your appreciation for the land and life.

• Let children experience nature. The structure and basic stability of nature is picked up subtly by children and will provide an underlying confidence that there is order to life beyond the sometimes fallible institutions of humankind. This formative experience can make the difference between hanging on or going crazy in times of stress.

These interactions with the world outside the human sphere are like threads connecting us to our survival. The stronger we make our connections and the greater the number of people who are motivated to develop their contact, the stronger will be the bond between humanity and the Earth that supports us.

• As our values evolve around respect for environmental reality, some very interesting changes take place in the way things appear. A classic example can be found in the way one might view a $50,000 car. We have been trained to be impressed by such a flashy item. However, considering that the basic need served by a car can be provided for a great deal less money, it is at least as appropriate to sympathize with the owner. If his or her self image requires large expenditures just to feel good about themselves or to "look good" to others, she or he could probably use some moral support.

73

Social Action

• Individual actions and attitudes are the elements from which societies are made. The governing policies of countries, where not overly modified by the cunning and coercion of particular interest groups, are a reflection of the individual attitudes which make up the society.

It is our right to influence the direction in which society goes. Between one third and one half of all the paid work we do is directed through taxes into the actions of Governments. This wealth, and the additional power the institutions gain through authority, belong to everyone.

Sustainability has to become a design criteria of institutional policy. We can bring this about by making the goal of sustainability widely known. It is not necessary to tell people we have to become sustainable. We only need to bring the option to their attention. When they think about it, the reality of the situation will speak more clearly than anything we can say. The sustainability cards described at the back of the book are particularly effective because they are unobtrusive and easily stored for future reference.

Many people can be reached through clubs, associations and religious institutions. If you have access to any of these, introduce the topic at a local meeting and ask that group to introduce the issue to the parent organization for consideration by all the local groups. These networks of citizens groups are probably the most effective way to reach out and are well worth any frustrating delays and procedures you might have to go through to access them. With bigger organizations, like the churches and service clubs, response may not come until contact is made through several local groups. When the connection is made,

74

however, their networks spread across the continent and around the globe.

The word can also be spread by writing letters to local papers, community leaders and elected representatives.

Once the population knows what sustainability means, the politicians will respond or others will take their places.

There has been widespread acceptance of the Brundtland Commission's definition of sustainability. The time has come to extend the debate into more detail. If anyone takes issue with one Guidepost or another, they can explain how they think we can overcome the environmental crisis otherwise. Everyone involved in such discussions will be wiser for the experience.

Political action we can press for

• Protection of long-term resource use. Measures must be taken to balance the long-term value of sustainable resource use against the immediate value of exhaustive short-term exploitation.

• Taxation of resource use rather than income.

A certain amount of money is necessary to run a country, but where the money is taken from is a matter of choice. Decisions about what is taxed and what is not taxed play a significant role in how a country develops. Much would change if taxes were drawn on the use of resources rather than on personal income.

• Resource intensive goods would become more expensive and labour intensive ones would become less expensive.

75

- **Individuals would have more money to spend, thereby stimulating the economy.**

- **There would be more jobs because the labour component of production would cost less.**

- **Restoration and repair for reuse would also be encouraged resulting in more work and less garbage.**

- **More care and artistry could be afforded thereby producing better quality and more esthetic goods.**

- **Goods which last would have even greater appeal.**

- **The use of recycled materials could be encouraged by taxing them less than newly extracted resources.**

- **Respect would be cultivated for the limitation of natural resources and for the impact of their removal.**

- Citizen access to environmental information. Universal access to environmental information can enable individuals to develop their understanding of any part of the problem and join in the effort to bring about solutions.

- The use of security budgets to address current as well as potential threats to security. Our security is threatened by the environmental crisis. If the budgets of our security institutions do not substantially address this serious situation, their mandates should be reexamined. We direct a generous portion of our tax money toward security. It would be tragic if our well-being was undermined while the institution paid to protect us was looking elsewhere for an enemy.

- Increased citizen involvement in decision making. Call for the right of any people effected by a decision to be involved in making that decision.

• Sustainability labeling. Call for the labeling of goods with some form of sustainability index so that, as consumers, we can make clear choices for the most sustainable options.

• Encourage the adoption of political jurisdictions coinciding with bioregional boundaries.

One major obstacle to solving environmental problems is that the jurisdiction over territories needing management is often shared by different political bodies. This leads to a great deal of confusion and inhibits the effectiveness of measures to care for the territory. Since different water sheds, climatic regions, forests and agricultural regions will always need coherent management to assure their sustainability, we should introduce these considerations whenever jurisdictional boundaries come up for review.

• Recently Canada had an extensive public debate about updating its constitution. It could have been a perfect opportunity to work the long-term care and maintenance of the environment into the social structure.

What is a country if not the land and life and the people living from them? A constitution outlines the relationship of a people to their territory and to each other. It is supposed to provide a coherence as generations come and go. Clearly, this provides an ideal place to institute the principles of sustainability. Canada chose not to change its constitution in the manner proposed. When the topic comes up again, in Canada or elsewhere, we should grasp the opportunity to look beyond immediate interests and lay a foundation to guide us through the long term future.

• Encourage population responsiveness. If we succeed in finding environmental balance, civilization could last for hundreds of thousands of years. Climatic and geological changes over that time will likely effect the number of people the Earth can support. A mature civilization would want to predict such changes and gradually adjust for them rather than ignore them and suffer major calamities.

• Tree Day. Press for the designation of a national holiday during which people would be encouraged to plant and appreciate trees.

6

Our Common Future

The Report of the World Commission on Environment and Development (WCED). Also known as the Brundtland Commission.

In the fall of 1983, the General Assembly of the United Nations passed a resolution calling for the formation of an international commission to look into:

> **"the unprecedented growth in pressures on the global environment, and the grave predictions about the human future that were becoming commonplace."**

The Prime Minister of Norway at the time, Gro Harlem Brundtland was appointed as Chairman of the Commission. The Vice-Chairman was Mansour Khalid, deputy Prime Minister of the Sudan. Together, they selected 21 members equally representing the developed and the underdeveloped worlds.

When the Commission's report, *Our Common Future,* was presented to the world in 1987, it marked a turning point in history.

For more than two decades, various organizations and individuals have been warning us about the serious consequences of abusing our planet. Unfortunately, their messages were disregarded or discredited in preference of more conventional world views and vested interests. Not any more.

The credentials of the World Commission were beyond question. Made up of people from around the globe, all with impressive experience, the Commissioners included heads of state, ministers of environment, education, finance, marine affairs, research and technology, foreign affairs, justice, communications, agriculture, and urban affairs. Commissioners were scientists, diplomats, lawyers and professors of ecology, biology, zoology, soil science, agricultural chemistry, political science, engineering and law, and they had held senior positions in all manner of national and international organizations.

The scope of their inquiry was no less impressive. They traveled to all the continents and met with governments, industrial leaders, environmental groups and concerned individuals. They concluded that we are indeed faced with a crisis of proportions unparalleled in recorded history. Without a substantial change in our development process, we will seriously reduce the capacity of the Earth to support future generations.

With that said, the challenge of sustainability became official. Governments, industrial leaders, religious institutions and countless other organizations are taking another look at what is being said about the environment and our well-being. There is still an enormous amount of work to be done to spread an understanding of the situation and to adapt to it, but at least no one can fool people into inaction by arguing that the problem does not exist.

Our Common Future is published in paperback by the Oxford University Press.

An indication of how the Commission viewed the world situation is revealed through the following quotes from *Our Common Future*. They are reproduced here with the permission of the publisher.

"The changes in human attitudes that we call for depend on a vast campaign of education, debate, and public participation. This campaign must start now if sustainable human progress is to be achieved."

"Many present efforts to guard and maintain human progress, to meet human needs, and to realize human ambitions are simply unsustainable — in both the rich and poor nations. They draw too heavily, too quickly, on already overdrawn environmental resource accounts to be affordable far into the future without bankrupting those accounts. They may show profits on the balance sheets of our generation, but our children will inherit the losses. We borrow environmental capital from future generations with no intention or prospect of repaying. They may damn us for our spendthrift ways, but they can never collect on our debt to them."

"We are not forecasting a future; we are serving a notice — an urgent notice based on the latest and best scientific evidence — that the time has come to take the decisions needed to secure the resources to sustain this and coming generations."

"Poverty is a major cause and effect of global environmental problems. It is therefore futile to attempt to deal with environmental problems without a broader perspective that

81

encompasses the factors underlying world poverty and international equality."

"Poor people are forced to overuse environmental resources to survive from day to day, and their impoverishment of their environment further impoverishes them, making their survival ever more difficult and uncertain."

"A child born in a country where levels of material and energy use are high, places a greater burden on the Earth's resources than a child born in a poorer country. A similar argument applies within countries. Nonetheless, sustainable development can be pursued more easily when population size is stabilized at a level consistent with the productive capacity of the ecosystem."

"The coexistence of substantial military spending with unmet human needs has long evoked concern. President Eisenhower, for example, observed at the end of his term in office that 'every gun that is made, every warship launched, every rocket fired represents, in the final analysis, a theft from those who hunger and are not fed, who are cold and are not clothed'."

"Birth rates decline in industrial countries largely because of economic and social development. . . . Similar processes are now at work in developing countries. These should be recognized and encouraged. . . . But time is short, and developing countries will also have to promote direct measures to reduce fertility, to avoid going radically beyond the productive potential to support their populations."

"Renewable energy systems are still in a relatively primitive stage of development. But they offer the world potentially huge primary energy sources, sustainable in perpetuity and available in one form or another to every nation on Earth."

"The enforcement of common interests often suffers because areas of political jurisdictions and areas of impact do not coincide."

"Making the difficult choices involved in achieving sustainable development will depend on the widespread support and involvement of an informed public and of NGO's [Non-Government Organizations], the scientific community, and industry."

These quotations represent only a portion of the topics covered in *Our Common Future*. The contents include: the threat to our future, sustainable development, the international economy, population and human resources, food security, species and ecosystems, energy, industry, urban growth, oceans, space, Antarctica, peace, security, and institutional restructuring. In each section the authors develop the themes with a thoroughness only available from a global perspective, taking into account the views and concerns of rich and poor alike. In each area, they outline the work necessary to secure the future. In the end they say:

"The Commission realizes that such proposals may not appear politically realistic at this point in time. It believes, however, that — given the trends discussed in this report — the need to support sustainable development will become so imperative that political realism will come to require it."

How quickly this political realism comes of age depends on how hard we work to understand it ourselves and to impress it upon the people around us.

7

Working Together For Sustainability

If you share the concern for sustainability with a group of people, the following procedures for meeting, consensus and consultation, may be useful as you look for effective ways to work together.

Each of us has a large collection of experiences from which our thoughts and ideas spring. The experience present when a group of people gathers is far greater than that of any individual. With this greater experience to draw from, better and more effective action can be planned.

In both consensus and consultation, it can be helpful to meet in a circle. This allows every individual to see everyone else and to meet as equals. Also, a circle creates a space in the middle, into which all input can be directed and where the collective mind can be projected.

Consensus

Consensus is a procedure in which no decisions are made until everyone agrees on them, or if everyone does not agree, at least no one strongly objects. If, after a full and open discussion, anyone still has strong objections, they can block the decision and the matter is dropped.

The effectiveness of consensus comes from the fact that everyone has equal power in the process. No one is forced into anything that doesn't feel good to them. The actions decided on by the group have everybody's support, because everyone was involved in making the decision. Consensus works best with smaller groups where considerable trust and familiarity exist. It has been known to work in larger groups with impressive results, but large gatherings can get bogged down by the effort to please everyone. There is a tremendous sense of satisfaction when divergent views have been thoroughly worked through and a mutually satisfactory solution found. However, the process can take a lot of time, and in larger groups it's worth watching to make sure more people are not lost to the group through frustration than are persuaded to stay by attending at length to their divergent views.

Sometimes frustration levels can be minimized by having the key people involved in a difference of opinion go off together to work out common ground while the rest of the group proceeds with other business. When the conclusion from their deliberation is presented, it is often found to be satisfactory without requiring much additional time.

As long as sensitivity is maintained for those who want to get things done as much as for those with divergent views, consensus strengthens a group by confirming that everyone is important.

Consultation

Consultation is not to be confused with consultants or with situations where someone is consulted from outside of the group making a decision. What follows is a description of a particular meeting technique called consultation. It provides considerable direction on how to nurture collective thinking in order to gain the best possible understanding on which to base decisions and action.

Not all groups will want to open themselves as fully to a collective process as consultation suggests. The process aims to tap the synergetic wisdom which exists when a number of people come together for common cause.

The vision we need is more likely to arise in a group. Synergy is the tendency of whole things to be greater than the sum of their parts. An example close to home is your body. Bones, muscles, organs, blood and all the other parts, if studied independently, do not provide an understanding of who you are. Similarly, your group has a whole greater than the sum of its parts. There is also a synergy that exists among all people longing for a harmonious relationship with the Earth. Further strength can be gained from knowing that your group's sincerity will make it part of a much greater effort — an effort sufficient in its potential to meet and overcome the difficult challenge of our age. If your group is not comfortable with all the steps suggested here, use as much as you feel is useful.

Come together with confidence that there is a common solution to whatever questions you are going to discuss. As I mentioned earlier, a mental picture of what we want to achieve helps us find a way to get there.

Once the group is assembled, before embarking on the business of the gathering, it helps to take a few moments to focus your attention, to empower the spirit of the gathering. Sometimes holding hands to connect the circle for a few moments of silence is helpful. The mood of the meeting can be further guided by expressing the wish, silently or verbally, for guidance and inspiration from the whole greater than ourselves.

"Help us to make the best possible decisions for the effectiveness of the group, for the well being of the seventh generation and for all life on Earth."

So met, the gathering is ready to proceed. These four rules will guide discussion to more productive ends.

1. When an idea leaves a person's lips, it no longer belongs to the individual but becomes the possession of the circle.

Individuals let go of the ideas they offer, and comments are directed at the ideas and not at the people who happened to introduce them. Ideas can be too important to bear the baggage of individual personalities. Without this precaution good ideas are sometimes neglected for reasons that have no relationship to the ideas content.

Every effort should be made to avoid ridiculing anything that is presented. Intimidation of any sort will discourage people from offering divergent views and the whole group will be poorer for the loss of perspective. The precaution of separating ideas from the people who voice them creates a safe environment that encourages adherence to the second rule.

2. Participants are expected to express everything that comes to heart or mind on the topic being discussed, even

if it goes against what they themselves feel or the mood of the meeting.

This is sometimes called brain-storming. The mind in free-association can come up with ideas that have not been considered before. They are worth adding to the process. If any perspective on the topic goes unexpressed, the group will not have a full picture to work with and there is a chance that something important will be missed. If the topic of discussion has been seriously researched elsewhere, an effort should be made to include the research findings for consideration as well.

3. When conflicting views do arise, they are not to be avoided.

Differing opinions must come into contact so that the sparks of their confrontation can illuminate the truth of the matter. At these times, however, it is most important to remember that it is the ideas that are clashing and not the people. There is no harm in this sort of confrontation if the group has been diligent in detaching the ideas from the people; indeed, valuable insights can be gained from the exchange. Recall the wish at the commencement of the meeting for decisions to emerge that are best for all involved. If this wish is sincere, participants can watch the fireworks of the interaction in anticipation that the truth of the matter will emerge when all is said and considered.

4. If total agreement is not reached but a significant majority feel they have identified an appropriate course of action, dissenters are asked to go along with the plan.

The purpose of this is to avoid confusion about the decision when it is being implemented. If there is not total cooperation in implementing a decision, and the action fails, it will not be clear whether the failure was due to a wrong decision or to the lack of cooperation. The distinction is important for guiding future actions.

Since all perspectives are to be given due consideration at the time of the meeting, any shortcoming arising as the plan unfolds will be viewed in the light of the divergent views. If everyone is trying to make the plan work and it doesn't, it will be clear that something is wrong with the decision, and it can be reconsidered at another meeting.

Attitudes

In the tradition from which consultation arose, a number of attitudes have been identified that, if cultivated, can help people become increasingly effective in the process. These include:

- *Courtesy*; **listening with interest to all ideas expressed and speaking the content of one's own mind fully and with clarity.**

- *Aspiration*; **allowing and encouraging our better selves to dominate our weaknesses.**

- *Detachment*; **allowing equal respect for all views whether they come from our own lips or from someone else's.**

- *Humility*; **to remove the obstacle of one's own importance and thereby enable serious consideration of what others say.**

- *Patience*; **to hear all that is being said before forming judgments.**

- *Service*; **to accept the responsibility of looking for the truth by expressing all that comes to mind related to the topic and in turn listening to all opinions put forward.**

We are threatened today by a wide variety of environmental dangers. We need the synergistic strength of working together. By offering the best of our understandings and opening our minds to consider the offerings of others in the spirit of consultation, the collective wisdom of a group can emerge.

Think of our minds as the product of millions of years of development, our languages as a gift from thousands of years of communication and knowledge as the cumulative product of human experience. In this light, it is not so hard to see that what we accomplish with these tools is a part of something far greater than ourselves. By aligning ourselves with this greater whole, we will have the strength to make the future bright again.

8

Bioregionalism

Bioregionalism is a movement which encourages identification with the territories in which we live. Usually defined as the lands drained by a particular river system, bioregions would provide jurisdictional units that make ecological sense.

Bioregionalism contends that security begins by acting responsibly at home. If the people living in a particular region don't look after it, who will? It is a response to the tendency of industrial societies to lose touch with the territories in which they are located. This community of interest emphasizes sensitivity to the unique geographical and biological situations around us, as well as to the cultural heritage of local people. As we come to realize that lack of concern for the natural world is threatening our existence, more and more of us are inclined to preserve and to rehabilitate the regions where we live.

Bioregions are territories that share common natural features. They may be distinguished by a system of rivers that drain an area, or by a particular type of climate, soil or plant and animal life. The logic behind identifying one's territory by its natural features is that different bioregions require different sorts of care and offer different possibilities for the people living there. Having these things in common gives a unifying purpose to the people living in a region. By working together to protect and restore their own regions, people can regain a sense of belonging to a community and to the Earth.

A group seeking to re-establish a sense of regional identity and respect for the local ecology can start by looking into these things:

1. What are the distinguishing features of your bioregion?

2. What are the special local resources of the region?

3. How can the natural and cultural resources best be used and protected?

4. What exchanges of time and energy can people in the region make to best meet daily and long-term needs?

5. How can you enrich your children's knowledge of local and planetary issues?

Bioregionalism is also concerned with the wise use of human resources within a region. Indigenous peoples having lived directly from their territories for countless generations have a great deal to offer as we learn to care for the Earth. Everyone who puts a priority on sustainability will have something to contribute. All manner of customs, traditions, arts, skills and trades contribute to the cultural richness that can make a community vibrant and fulfilling. By aiming to supply a rich diversity of services within communities, by recycling resources, and by exchanging surpluses prudently with other regions, a territory can attempt to involve everyone with meaningful work. Bioregionalism looks within its territory to satisfy as many basic needs as possible, including education, health care and governance.

If people are to take their stewardship of the Earth seriously, electoral districts will eventually be defined along bioregional lines. The Brundtland report made it clear that, for a secure future, all development must take its environmental impact into account. With the exception of atmospheric and ocean pollution, which are clearly international concerns, environmental impact is the effect of something on the local bioregion. As people become increasingly concerned about these effects, a great many complications and disputes arise because actions in one jurisdiction affect the land and life of another. Most of these problems would be avoided if we defined our management units along bioregional lines.

What better, non-partisan reasons could there be for defining political boundaries? We must take the responsibility for the care and nurture of distinct regions. If these regions are not jurisdictional units, what institution will accommodate the common tasks of the people who live in them?

For further information on bioregionalism contact:

The New Catalyst
P.O. Box 189
Gabriola Island, B.C
V0R 1X0

Planet Drum
P.O. Box 31251
San Francisco, CA.
94131

9

Reasons For Hope

Can we prevent environmental collapse?

We face problems beyond the comprehension of any individual, yet the situation is far from hopeless. Hope comes from another quantity, even further beyond comprehension than the global environment — human creativity. One can barely imagine the extent of the creative ability of the people in a single town, let alone in a city or a whole country. Each person has perceptions, knowledge, imagination and the ability to act. Any individual who decides to work for sustainability can advance the cause. With dedication, one person can make a big difference. And there are millions and billions of people with more than enough reason to make a valiant effort. We all share a common future, and as our challenge becomes increasingly clear we will be able to count on people everywhere to do whatever they can.

Our eyes and ears together sense everything humanity does, our minds make all the decisions and our limbs direct all the work. It is not a question of our ability to adapt, only of our willingness to try. Is it our priority to make society sustainable?

Twenty billion people could probably live together on this planet for a while, but our existence would be fraught with hardship and would likely end with environmental collapse. On the other hand, 2,000 billion people, and more, could live here over the generations, taking turns in sustainable numbers, and all of them could have the opportunity for full and satisfying lives.

We have made remarkable progress in our efforts to keep up with the rapidly growing population. If we didn't have to double the amount of food and shelter available in the next generation, we would very quickly catch up with human need. Without pressing needs, the prospects of a peaceful world would increase considerably, and we wouldn't have the anxieties that lead to enormous military spending. Without spending hundreds of billions of dollars on arms, we would easily have the resources to provide the material security, health care and education that lead to population stability.

Where will the money come from to solve problems which once solved would free up enough money to solve them.

This riddle tests our civilization for intelligence and creativity.

We don't have to increase material production endlessly to maintain employment. As long as there are people in need, there will be work to do. If everyone has what they need and there is no work, we would have time to celebrate and to enjoy being alive until more work arises. Even so, "work" would likely take on a different meaning.

In anticipation of doubling populations and increasing demands, we have all been racing to keep up. The pressure of the "rat race" has made many people look at work as an undesirable part of life. With less than half as much needing to be done, the opportunity to provide goods or services for others might come to be seen more as a blessing than a chore.

Sustainability would result in a whole new attitude about being human. If everything we need could be provided with people working only three days a week, it stands to reason that three days work would be enough to pay for all we need. Unemployment would go down and the quality of life would improve. Free time would no longer be a luxury of the well-to-do. It would be a right. We would have enough time to give our children all the love they need to grow up strong and good, and time left over to give ourselves the opportunity to explore the greater potentials available to us as human beings.

Whatever it takes to accommodate the environmental reality of living on this planet, we will never lose the pleasures and wonders of creativity, sport and dance; of understanding and appreciating what we find around us; of relating to each other; and of humor, compassion and love. By managing the Earth sustainably, we will also gain peace of mind in knowing that our childrens' children will have the opportunity to enjoy their lives as well.

Surely the forests would be relieved if they only had to provide for the maintenance of buildings and the rejuvenation of cycling paper stocks. Likewise the soils would be relieved as we caught up with ourselves and were able to fulfill the responsibility of returning to them what we take away.

97

In the growth of an individual, there comes a point where we stop increasing in our physical size. If we didn't, our bodies would soon become unmanageable. As a civilization, we have been growing for thousands of years, involving ever greater quantities of the Earth's substance in our bodies, buildings, tools and toys. The environmental crisis clearly demonstrates that if we do not stop growing in size, civilization will become unmanageable.

As individuals, our physical maturation does not put an end to our personal development. In many ways we only begin to build our lives after the task of growing a mature body is complete. Similarly, when civilization stops growing it will not mean an end to our development. If we can stabilize our numbers and material desires before we cripple the environment, we will be able to look forward to a very promising future.

How do we make the decision to change?

It helps for a crisis to have a beginning. Rallying against aggression is relatively easy. The enemy can be clearly defined and a declaration of war establishes the social agenda.

The environmental situation is less clear. The crisis has crept up on us so quietly that there has been no distinct beginning to catch popular attention. And the "enemy," rather than being something separate from ourselves, at which to hurl all our destructive power, is closely intertwined with our own lives and has to be dealt with accordingly. Nonetheless, it is clear that we must overcome our non-sustainable customs and replace them with ways that are sustainable. The Brundtland Commission has served notice that this challenge is indeed upon us. We must now demand that the priority be declared.

Pressing need is not the only reason that wars are successful at involving people. For many, war offers an opportunity for adventure, for the feeling that every bit of one's abilities are called into action. There are many accounts of people who, even while recognizing the horrors, found they missed the intensity of the experience after they returned home. Another thing people have missed after returning from war is the companionship felt between those who shared the challenge.

The struggle for sustainability can offer these same opportunities. If it is adventure you long for, there is no shortage of that in store. It is a brave and heroic act to face one's inner self and undertake change. Similarly, great ingenuity will be required to address our economic and social institutions in ways that will inspire cooperation rather than reaction. After all, armies, secret police and even thugs, organized to help powerful interests exploit the Earth, are not all figures from the past. There is challenge enough for the bravest of souls, and the stakes are higher than they have been at any time in history.

Companionship will also be easy to find, as we form alliances to tackle the issues in our communities. Watch the local paper for stories about a waste dump proposal, attempts to start up recycling programs, a campaign to stop development on good farm land or any other local environmental issue. It is your call to action. The newspaper office can tell you how to find the people involved. They need your help. Put yourself into the effort, and you will find friendships which can last a lifetime.

If you can't find an existing group that you feel comfortable with, pass the Guideposts material around in circles where you do feel comfortable. You are sure to find others who share your concerns, with whom you can undertake some constructive activities. There are many established groups that can provide pointers on ways to become active if a course of action is not already clear.

Perhaps you are already a part of a mutual interest group. How do your friends feel about sustainability? Your parents or children, your church, temple or synagogue? How about the people you work with, or those at your club? Take this book or the Guideposts video to those people and present them with the challenge. Ask them if they agree that we need to become sustainable. Have them look at each other and realize that they are not alone in their concern. For every person you can find, there are thousands of others who are no less concerned and no less willing to act if they can see cause for hope. Together they are themselves cause for hope.

* * *

Few people actually disagree with the Guideposts definition of sustainability. Still, there is a hesitancy to place sustainability clearly within the moral imperatives of good and bad. Sustainable activities are good, non-sustainable activities are bad. Perhaps we hesitate because we know that when we do acknowledge this value, leading a "good" life will require far-reaching change. We also know that there is no acceptable choice but to make those changes. While we are not responsible for how the world has come to us, we do have a responsibility to choose the most sustainable options currently available and to open our hearts and minds to inspirations that may reveal still more sustainable opportunities.

Much of our ability to act is entrusted to governments. They are supposed to maintain the integrity of society. Do your elected representatives care about sustainability? They say so, no doubt, but do they really know what sustainability means? Do they press for and support appropriate legislation and planning decisions? Billions of dollars of our money is at their disposal. Our elected representatives should be leading us to sustainability — or we have to replace them with people who will. If your representatives don't respond to your suggestions, find a respected individual in your community who understands and supports the goal, encourage them to enter the political process, then let your community know that person will work for a sustainable future.

We need laws that discourage and prohibit non-sustainable activities and others which encourage and reward sustainable ones. Such laws would clarify the direction unmistakably. They would further strengthen our personal responsiveness and would turn the hands of those who might overlook moral values for other interests.

Ultimately, however, if we are to put the environmental crisis behind us once and for all, we must instill the value of sustainability deeply within our hearts. We must feel it as clearly as we feel the need to care for our children. Indeed, becoming sustainable is caring for our children.

10

History of The "Guideposts"

In the early 1970s, the *Institute for the Study of Cultural Evolution* (ISCE) began an inventory of the concerns and aspirations of people voluntarily working for a better world.

Where are we heading? Where should we be heading? What do you know about the way in which society changes? These were the questions we asked across Canada and the US. Notes were made of the responses and from recommended literature. After four years, all the notes were sorted by similarities and the resulting categories identified the Guideposts — a common denominator of popular concern and vision.

As a statement of direction, the Guideposts provide an important service. People worry when they feel our institutions are not rising to the challenge of the times. When they look around to see what other options there are, they find movements focusing on environment, development, peace, justice and getting the most out of being human. It is not always clear that these concerns are all parts of the same vision and much new energy is lost to uncertainty about choosing among them.

As a goal, sustainability includes all these movements. When people are looking for a direction that makes more sense than the social goals we have outgrown, sustainability offers one alternative with many well-developed branches. Confident that there is a clear option, people can respond to their concerns by looking into the component movements to see where their skills and interests fit.

* * *

The other focus of the ISCE study was on how societies change. Two ideas have played key roles in developing the Guideposts approach. One is about how new areas of understanding unfold, the other about how individuals develop their understanding. The first can be illustrated by an analogy made between the exploration of unfamiliar territories and the evolution of words in a language.

Map of Words

To the European explorers the Americas were unknown. One expedition could spend an entire season traveling up the coast to see what they could see. If, late in the season, they discovered a large river pouring into the ocean, they could take a reading on the stars and record where the mouth of that river was. The next year they could go straight to that place and spend the entire season exploring the river.

With points of interest similarly located along the river, any navigator with the charts could set out and travel directly to the place of their choice.

So it is with words. When objects, phenomena and ideas are identified, we mark them with words. When someone else wants to learn about the same things, they can start by learning the words that identify the subject matter and go on from there.

Sustainability is one of these words. Its definition marks the territory, so anyone who learns the term can recognize the basic consideration. Having the territory symbolized by a single word makes it easier to think and communicate about the concern it represents.

Frame of Reference

The other idea central to this project has to do with how understanding develops. A frame of reference is a pattern around which one can arrange experiences and ideas. The pattern indicates the relationship between the considerations involved. If the experiences and information we come across in our lives fit within the frame of reference, the overview is reinforced and we start to understand the basic situation.

The value of a frame of reference became clear to me at a roller derby. I'd never heard of the sport when someone gave me a free ticket. As I watched I was unable to make sense of what I saw. Two teams roller-skated around a heavily banked track as fast as they could. Every now and then they would all stop skating and a score would be recorded. I couldn't figure out how the points were being made.

During intermission I asked a cameraman what was happening. He explained the rules of the game. When the action started again, the formation made sense, I could identify the strategies, see when a point was coming and had the satisfaction of knowing when and for whom it would be recorded.

The rules of the game provided a frame of reference which I could use to assess what I was seeing.

Our environmental situation is a good deal more complex than a roller derby, but it is not beyond the comprehension of people with average intelligence and moderate interest. The *Guideposts for a Sustainable Future* provide a frame of reference.

If this observation is accurate, widespread provision of the Guideposts frame of reference will enable a lot of people to comprehend the environmental situation and recognize problems and solutions when they encounter them. When these people have collected enough information around the basic understanding, they will also be able to initiate corrective actions on their own.

* * *

For a few years after the Guideposts were refined they were identified with a word from the tradition of the Hopi nation. The Hopi are generally acknowledged by other indigenous North Americans as the first people to have inhabited the continent. The context from which the word comes reflects our circumstances today. In traditions that have been passed down for thousands of years, the Hopi recount the story of the destruction of their civilization on three occasions. Each disaster followed the same basic pattern. The people started out living in the natural environment, intercepting the flows of matter and energy and living from them. They successfully increased their population and built up their settlements. This growth continued until their material culture became so extensive that people were immersed in their own works and lost contact with the natural world. Actions were taken without regard for the life-supporting processes of nature.

In each cycle there were individuals within the culture who were still aware or who had become aware of the natural processes and who realized the folly of living in ignorance of them. They separated themselves from the larger centers and were able to avoid the fall of their civilization.

Then, as now, people were so involved in human creations that many did not understand or consider the natural processes by which life is maintained on Earth.

The first world was destroyed be fire, the second by ice, and the third by flooding. In the last instance, the people who had left mainstream culture to regain a sensitivity to the ways of nature, gathered up reeds that grew in the area and made boats to ride out the flood. They reached North America, migrated around the continent for a number of generations and eventually settled in the area of Arizona where their descendants are living today.

"Bakavi" (ba ka vé) was the name of the reeds from which their boats were made.

Unfortunately we discovered people were often wary of the unusual word.

Today, *Guideposts for a Sustainable Future* says in five English words exactly what Bakavi was meant to say.

11

Environmental Problems

In Chapter 4, the relationship between ecology and economics was presented, dividing environmental problems into the categories of: problems of tolerance and problems of resource supply. The problems described briefly here follow the same order. Notice that destruction of Aboriginal cultures, militarism and overpopulation are listed separately since they are implicated with both sets of problems.

The follow chapter is not fun to read. It summarizes a complex of problems that have taken billions of people and many decades if not centuries to create. To an individual they can be overwhelming but ignoring them will not help. Remember as you read that there are many millions of people to help correct the situation.

Problems of tolerance are presented here first because, if they are left unchecked, we will poison ourselves before we exhaust resource supplies. Nevertheless, all the issues are part of the same crisis. The work will not be done as long as any of them remain unresolved.

PROBLEMS OF TOLERANCE

Acid Rain

Acid rain is caused by the introduction of sulfur and nitrogen oxides into the air, primarily from the burning of coal, gasoline and oil. When these elements combine with water vapor, they form sulfuric and nitric acids. This produces mist, fog, snow and rain that is acidic. The situation is unusual for most of the life on Earth today and produces a number of problems:

• in *fresh water*, the acidity of lakes and streams that receive large amounts of acid rain (and melted acid snow) can rise to intolerable levels for plants and fish. This is why many water bodies downwind or downstream from major polluters are practically devoid of life.

• in *soils*, when soil acidity rises, it changes the conditions in which soil micro-organisms live. Furthermore, the acid in the soil will dissolve substances like lead or mercury that are normally inert. These are then absorbed by both soil-life and plants, affecting them and the associated food chain adversely.

• in *the air*, acidic mists and fogs are thought to be responsible for some deterioration of forests. Acidity of this kind also causes or aggravates respiratory difficulties when we breath the moist air.

• on *property*, numerous structures deteriorate when repeatedly exposed to acidic precipitation. Limestone buildings and monuments are notable among these.

The Greenhouse Effect

Glass is transparent to the energy of sunlight but not to heat. Therefore, when light shines into a greenhouse and warms things inside, the heat is held in, and the temperature inside goes up, even when it is cold outside. In the atmosphere, carbon dioxide and some other gases produced by human activities and some natural processes have the same property as glass, in that they let light through and hold heat in.

Carbon dioxide is the major by-product of burning oil, gas, coal and wood. The enormous volumes of these fuels we have burned has raised the amount of carbon dioxide in the atmosphere by close to 50 percent since pre-industrial times. As a result, we are increasing the temperature of the planet and changing weather patterns. It has been calculated that, at present rates of fuel consumption, by the year 2020 the average global temperature may have risen by as much as 4 degrees Celsius.

The dangers of this situation are several: changing climates would seriously affect many life forms that would find themselves in conditions for which they are not adapted. This includes some forests and customary field crops. Food production problems would be further aggravated as many dry areas would become dryer and unfamiliar plant diseases could find suitable climates and affect crops in territories where they were not a problem before. Rising temperatures may also melt the polar ice fields, raising sea levels and flooding large areas of the world's best farm land and many coastal cities. This would cause enormous dislocation if allowed to continue unchecked.

Ozone Depletion

The stratosphere is a layer in the atmosphere located between 15 and 50 kilometers above us. Within this area there is a considerable amount of ozone gas. It is the ozone in the stratosphere that filters out the harsh ultra-violet rays of the sun, preventing them from reaching the Earth's surface where they can cause skin cancers, eye cataracts, crop damage and otherwise harm living things.

We have become accustomed to using a group of chemicals that can drift up into the stratosphere and break down the protective layer of ozone. These chemicals, known as chlorofluorocarbons or CFCs, are a principal substance in refrigerators and air conditioners. Chlorofluorocarbons are also used as cleansers for electronic circuit boards, propellants in some aerosol sprays and in the manufacture of such items as extruded Styrofoam insulation and some foam packaging materials. Automobile air conditioning units are particularly dangerous as the temperature changes and vibration to which they are regularly subjected can lead to the escape of their CFCs.

The appearance of holes in the ozone layer, first over the Antarctic and later in the Arctic region, and an estimated 5 percent reduction in the layer overall, has caused international alarm. On September 16, 1987, history was made in Montreal when most of the nations of the world met to establish the first-ever international environmental protocol — to regulate ozone depleting chemicals. They agreed to reduce the production of these substances to 50 percent of 1986 levels by 1999.

It takes quite a while for CFCs to drift into the upper atmosphere. This means much of what we have produced so far has yet to reach that level. Once CFCs are exposed to ultra-violet radiation in the stratosphere, they are broken down, freeing their chlorine which, in turn, reduces O_3 molecules (ozone) into regular oxygen molecules that do not block ultra-violet radiation. Every year about 20 percent of the free chlorine in the stratosphere drifts to lower levels, gets caught up in rain and is washed out of harm's way. Some researchers say that we need an immediate 80 percent reduction of CFCs to reverse the deterioration of the ozone layer. The international agreement is a start, but much more is needed.

Municipal Waste

Consumers in industrial societies purchase a great quantity and variety of goods. Almost all of them are eventually thrown away. However, we are coming to realize that there is no "away." The accumulation of our waste products on the land, in the water and in the air creates a number of problems — problems of bulk, toxicity and aesthetics.

Bulk: With garbage being produced at a rate greater than three pounds per person per day, multiplied by millions of people, the volumes are mountainous. Old dump sites are being filled up, and wherever new sites are proposed, local populations mobilize to stop them. It has become very difficult and costly to establish new landfill sites. Reduction, Reuse and Recycling are the first line of defense against garbage volume.

Toxicity: Many of the "wonder-products" of the modern era are made from dangerous substances. If these

111

are thrown out with household garbage, they end up in the same dump with everything else. Their containers break down and the toxic materials soak into the ground where they can disrupt local life and pollute water supplies. Anything that is marked with warnings of toxicity should be put in a safe place until it can be processed in a toxic waste disposal program.

Organic waste from kitchens and gardens can add to the problem. As they decompose in a garbage heap they can form organic acids that can dissolve and react with harmful materials which might otherwise have stayed put.

Aesthetics: Many people are still thoughtlessly throwing packaging materials and containers away wherever they remove the contents. Wind blown garbage litters the landscape, particularly around landfill sites. These areas are further depreciated by the noisy and hazardous traffic of garbage trucks and by scavenger birds, rats and other vermin.

Energy from Waste

Deriving energy from waste has been proposed as a solution to waste problems. Unfortunately, burning garbage can lead to other serious problems. When the gases from such fires rise in the smokestacks, they often recombine and create dangerous substances, notably the highly toxic dioxins. These by-products are then spread by the wind over the surrounding territory. By the time hundreds of thousands and even millions of dollars have been spent building an incinerator, it is hard to consider not using it. Additionally, the newspapers and cardboard that keep incinerator fires hot are no longer available for recycling.

Industrial Waste

By-products of production are another large category of waste. These materials are not a part of finished products but are either used in, or result from the production of products. By-products accumulate at the factories where they are created and need disposal. For years these substances were buried at landfill sites, piped into rivers, dumped into the ocean and otherwise thoughtlessly discarded.

Hundreds of old dump sites have been identified. Others that had been forgotten, turn up from time to time, as containers break down and ground water supplies become contaminated.

Partly because of the harm caused by such practices, awareness has grown about the need to isolate dangerous materials from the environment. Legislation has been passed in many places regulating the disposal of toxic materials, and the companies involved have responded in a number of ways:

• New methods of production have been developed that generate less toxic by-products.

• In some cases, "waste exchange" programs have been implemented to help one company find another company that can use some of their waste as raw material in another production process.

• Methods have been devised to detoxify some substances, or to render them solid and insoluble so they cannot enter the water cycles.

• Other techniques have been developed to destroy toxic materials, often through burning at high temperatures.

Transport of Toxic Wastes

Unless a company is big enough to have their own disposal facilities on site, they have to transport their waste to suitable facilities elsewhere. Accidents along transport routes have led to serious problems. A new wave of legislation is developing, aimed at improving transport safety and making sure that clean-ups are carried out quickly when spills do occur.

Not all efforts by industry to deal with their toxic materials have been in good faith. Some have simply moved their factories to countries that do not have pollution control laws. Others have arranged to export their waste materials to countries where people are not yet aware of the hazards, or the government is willing to allow the import and dumping of toxic substances in exchange for much-needed hard currency. Some international regulations are in place to protect unsuspecting people, but further measures are needed. In the global environment it is not much help to outlaw a polluting industry at home and then purchase its products from next door.

Part of the solution to the industrial waste problem will come from conscientious consumers. There is a movement afoot to provide information about the environmental impact of different products. The "Environmental Choice" program in Canada is a small start. Products that pass an evaluation can display this label to notify consumers that they are "Planet Friendly." However, judging what is and is not planet friendly has proven politically troublesome.

Considerable public pressure will have to come to bear before a full sustainability index will be required labeling on products offered for sale. Such an indicator would show how the product rates when it is disposed of responsibly as well as when disposal is careless. Until then, if we want to be environmentally responsible in what we buy, we will have to keep an ear open to the advice of citizens' environmental groups.

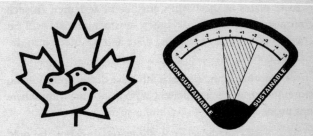

Nuclear Waste

Of all the toxic wastes produced by industry, radioactive materials deserve a category of their own. They are unique because of the length of time over which they can present a hazard; some are dangerous for as long as several hundred thousand years.

There is also the danger that small amounts of certain nuclear wastes could be made into nuclear bombs by terrorist groups or sovereign nations. In either case, their use could have grave repercussions for everyone on Earth.

115

Nuclear Waste Disposal

Since it is impossible to be sure what will transpire over tens of thousands of years, there are no proven methods for disposing of nuclear waste. The methods being considered include:

• Deep burial in solid rock formations thought to be safe from earthquake activity or ground water circulation.

• Dropping it into deep ocean trenches where two massive plates of the Earth's crust come together. In such circumstances, the theory goes, waste materials will be covered over by the advancing plate and be drawn into the Earth's core.

• Another plan, and currently the default policy, is to store nuclear waste indefinitely in pools of water near where it is produced.

Disposal of radioactive waste materials is not the only process in which the nuclear industry produces dangerous by-products. There are hazards associated with mining, refining, transport and use as well.

It is generally recognized that any increase in the level of radiation in the environment increases the incidence of cancer. What the experts are trying to figure out is, to what extent can increasing cancer rates be justified by the enormous amount of power available from nuclear reactors?

Nuclear Liability

There have been no new orders for nuclear reactors in the USA for many years now, but the situation is different in Canada. Before reactors were built in Canada, the industries lobbied for a piece of legislation known as the

Nuclear Liabilities Act. This Act limits the liability of companies involved in building reactors to 75 million dollars, assuring that they won't be bankrupted if a serious accident occurs. The companies are well protected, but the people who live within 500 miles or so of the reactors cannot be insured. Try asking your insurance agent about nuclear accident insurance.

Since the nuclear industry spends millions of dollars telling everyone how safe their product is, it seems they ought to prove their faith by assuming liability for accidents, as any other industry does.

Decommissioning

One other problem with nuclear installations that has received very little attention is decommissioning. As with any other equipment, nuclear reactors wear out. There is a planned usefulness of 30 to 40 years for reactors. After that time, in addition to the used fuel, there is an entire apparatus that must be disposed of. Much of it will be highly radioactive and will require special remote-controlled procedures for disassembly. As with the spent fuel, a disposal site must be found where the pieces won't pose any problems for some thousands of years.

Some people estimate the cost of decommissioning at nearly half the cost of construction, yet there is little money being put aside from the sale of nuclear power to pay for disposal of the plants.

A special committee of the Canadian Government has recommended a moratorium on the construction of new nuclear plants until the problems of waste storage are solved.

Food Irradiation

Another concern in the radiation category is food irradiation. This is a method of preserving food by exposing it to radiation from certain nuclear by-products. There are many inadequately answered questions about the effectiveness and safety of the process. Public pressure has kept plants from setting up in Canada, but we do import irradiated mangoes, papayas and shrimp from Thailand and yams from the Ivory Coast.

Water Pollution

Water, as we know, is the major component in all living things. When water becomes contaminated, it can carry contaminants into the life processes of anything that lives.

Dumping waste directly into lakes and rivers, burial in old mines or deep wells, landfilling and emitting gases into the air, are all ways in which toxic materials find their way into the water cycles. Once water is polluted, the contamination can travel wherever the water does. Toxic materials deposited in one spot can travel for hundreds and even thousands of miles in weather patterns, ocean currents and the movement of ground and surface water, to affect life processes far away.

Eutrophication has been a major problem with water bodies. This occurs when quantities of sewage or fertilizers from agricultural run-off are present. When sewage decomposes, or when the algae and other plant life that grow abundantly on the sewage and agricultural run-off die and decompose, a rapidly growing population of decomposing bacteria can take up all the oxygen in the water, thereby killing most of the other things living there.

There have been some encouraging signs. For example, the Thames River in England and Lake Erie, between Canada and the USA, were both extremely polluted, but after concerted clean-up efforts, they again support life.

Clean-up is possible by eliminating the dumping of raw sewage into waterways, proper disposal of industrial waste and careful farming practices.

Ground water contamination is a more difficult problem. Whereas lakes and rivers turn over their contents relatively quickly, ground water moves very slowly, sometimes as little as one or two kilometers a year. This means that once an area is contaminated, it can take decades or even centuries to be flushed clean after the source of contamination is removed. For the thousands of people whose wells have been contaminated, there is no solution but to bring in water from elsewhere and to raise people's awareness to minimize occurrences in other places.

Pesticides

When we talk about pollution from landfill sites, vehicle exhausts and industrial processes, we are usually looking at substances whose harmful effects were not anticipated. Pesticides, on the other hand, are chosen because they are poisonous. Also they are spread intentionally by the ton over large tracts of fields and forest. This practice produces many hazards.

• It is not uncommon for pesticide residues to be found on the foods we buy. It is a little more surprising to know that through the cycling of water and the interconnections of the food chain, pesticides and their residues have been distributed everywhere on Earth. A classic example is DDT. Although its use has been banned for a decade or more in many industrial countries, it can still be found in virtually all foods and living things.

• Farm workers who are exposed while applying pesticides or working in recently treated fields, have suffered unusual illnesses and even death. Cancer, respiratory disorders and birth defects are just a few of the hazards of exposure.

• Pesticides and their residues can combine with other substances and produce other toxins.

• Awareness of the harmful side effects of pesticides has grown considerably over the last two decades. Many developed countries have banned or severely restricted the use of some of the most dangerous ones. It is to the industrial world's dishonour however, that even with proof of unacceptable dangers, many of these substances are still produced and sold in large quantities to Third World countries. Besides putting the people at risk in those countries, the poisons are often used on crops that are then sold to and distributed back in the developed nations: the "boomerang effect."

• Cases have been frequently documented where pests have developed resistance to the poisons used on them. This often leads to the use of increasingly heavier doses and sometimes requires that one pesticide be replaced with a more powerful one.

• Most agricultural poisons not only kill the pest they are aimed at, but also the creatures that usually eat those pests. Without natural enemies, when the pest returns, it can multiply even faster and cause much more damage before the farmer is able to respond.

"Pesticides don't know when to stop killing" warns the International Pesticide Action Network.

Environmental Illness

Sometimes called "Twentieth Century Disease." environmental illness is a consequence of living in a polluted world.

Our immune systems have developed over millions of years to protect us from substances and organisms that get into our bodies. In the relatively consistent conditions of the past, we have been well equipped to deal with most intrusions. This century, however, many thousands of new substances have been added to the environment. Our immune systems don't recognize these previously unknown intruders, and do not always deal with them well.

Some symptoms of environmental illness are: frequent headaches, rashes, brief loss of memory, difficulty with concentration, unexplained mood swings, dizziness, continual lack of energy, nose bleeds, coughs, and respiratory problems. It appears that the body can cope with strange new substances up to a point, but once that point is passed it can no longer prevent reactions. Furthermore, the immune system appears to get "confused." and it will set off reactions that encumber rather than help the person involved. Once the physiological confusion sets in, it can severely impair an individual's ability to lead a normal life.

Relief from this illness, and sometimes the cure, requires that sufferers avoid substances that cause their bodies to react. Pesticide residues, food additives, processed and synthetic foods are often part of the problem. Synthetic materials in living quarters, some carpets and cloth, and many building materials can play a part, as can solvents and some cleaning products. In addition, there are pollutants carried in the air and water. All in all, it requires a major effort to provide relief from symptoms that can range from mild irritations to severe attacks of asthma, kidney shutdown and other potentially fatal reactions.

Relief, however, can lead to a relaxation of the confused body processes and sometimes to recovery of the ability to cope with much of what is considered today to be a normal environment.

People suffering from environmental illnesses are often hard to diagnose, leaving them dependent on family, friends or welfare systems, as they try to deal with their complex situations. Part of the difficulty in being diagnosed and even in having environmental illness acknowledged, is because the symptoms are so varied and often intermittent. Some frustrated victims fear that the lack of recognition is a "conspiracy"; for authorities to acknowledge environmental illness would be to inform a sizable portion of the population that their lives are contaminated. Public health repercussions of such an acknowledgment would reach deeply into our industrial economy and put multi-billion dollar interests up for scrutiny.

PROBLEMS OF RESOURCE LIMITATIONS

Depletion Of Soil Quality

The health of a society ultimately depends on the health of its soils. We have a number of causes for concern:

Loss of Nutrients

When plants grow, certain of their nutrient requirements are absorbed from the soil. When they are harvested and taken away from where they grew, the nutrients they absorbed go with them, seldom to return. Chemical fertilizers are then brought in to supplement natural soil fertility, rarely containing anything but the three major nutrients — nitrogen, potassium and phosphorous. Consequently, the availability of trace minerals and other soil elements slowly declines.

A further problem with the use of chemical fertilizers is that they discourage micro-organisms in the soil, which normally replenish fertility. Not only are these organisms undernourished for lack of organic matter, they can be killed or actively suppressed in their natural functions by the concentrated chemicals.

This combination of factors leads to an increase in the amount of chemical fertilizer needed each year, if yields are to be maintained. The cost of this increasing input has led a growing minority of farmers to discover that they can make more money over the long term by returning to non-chemical methods of crop production. The transition is difficult to make, however, because it takes a number of years for soil to recover from chemical practices.

123

Soil Compaction

The yield of food per farmer has gone up considerably because of mechanization, but as farm equipment becomes bigger and bigger, a new problem develops. Soil compaction occurs where soil particles are pressed closer together by the weight and vibration of heavy equipment, and by the working of moist soil in which the particles settle together more easily. These factors are aggravated by a hard-pressed layer, called a "plow sole", which develops at the level where the bottom of a conventional plow rides below the surface year after year. The result is that it is more difficult for water and air to enter the soil. Water collects on the surface resulting in surface run-off and erosion. The roots of plants also find it harder to penetrate compacted soil, so they have less access to the moisture and nutrients from deeper levels. Compaction is less of a problem where there are greater amounts of organic matter in the soil.

Wind and Water Erosion

Plants and plant matter on the land surface protect it from wind, cushion the impact of rain drops and hold water during storms, so it can soak slowly into the Earth. The roots of plants bind the soil together, making it more stable under adverse conditions. Without a surface covering, soil is subject to erosion. Muddy water flowing in the creeks and clouds of dust blowing through the air indicate the loss of soil fertility. Soil that has been building up for thousands of years can be lost in a single generation of mismanagement. Such damage is extensive throughout the world and is cause for great concern.

Salinization

In dry areas the problem of salts building up in the soil is natural. This happens when ground water is near enough to the surface to rise up and evaporate, leaving its salt content behind in increasing concentrations. Certain modern agricultural practices increase this occurrence significantly.

• When native, year-round vegetation is replaced with seasonal crops that do not use as much water, the water table rises, and there are more places where the water can reach the surface and evaporate.

• The custom of leaving land fallow for a season has the same effect.

• Salinization is also a problem on irrigated lands where more water is used than the plants can absorb. The remainder evaporates, leaving its salts behind.

On the Canadian prairies, salinization is currently estimated to cost farmers over a quarter billion dollars a year and is increasing at a rate of about 10 percent each year.

Although the growing of food is taken for granted by much of the industrialized world, it is a matter of utmost importance. If we cannot recognize the vital resource of healthy soil and take measures to stop and reverse its degradation, food production will claim our attention in an unpleasant manner.

Soil Loss To Urban Expansion

The other major cause of soil loss is the spread of urban centers. This is particularly serious, because most successful cities got their start from the wealth produced by the rich agricultural land surrounding them. As a result the best land for growing food is also the most likely to be paved and built over.

In Ontario over the last 25 years, 80 percent of all urban expansion has been over agricultural land. This is a problem experienced around the world.

Deforestation

In our continuing search for land to grow food on, and for trees to make lumber and paper, we have cut down well over half of all the forested areas on Earth.

Problems of deforestation include: loss of habitat for forest animals, increased runoff, consequent soil erosion, silting up of streams and dammed areas, dropping water tables, and changes in weather patterns.

When individual trees are cut and removed from a forest, other trees grow to fill in the space; little changes in the forest community. However, when entire areas are clear-cut, leaving no trees of any size, whole communities of animals, birds, plants and insects can no longer find the conditions they need to live. It can take decades or even centuries for such areas to reestablish themselves.

When forest cover is removed, the soil no longer receives the protection of layers of leaves, needles and twigs that cushioned the fall of rain drops and held water while it soaked into the ground. Instead, storm water will tend to run over the surface of the earth, and without the trees' roots to hold it together, much soil can be dislodged and washed down the slopes. This process has compounded the loss of fertility on the slopes with filling-in of water bodies downstream. There are cases where the reservoirs of large dams have been filled in, causing great losses in hydro-electric and irrigation potentials. With less water soaking into the ground, the level of underground water reserves can drop, causing other problems. Another hazard is that, without the canopy of forest leaves catching carbon dioxide and transpiring water back into the atmosphere, local weather patterns can change, sometimes for the worse.

It looks as though deforestation took its toll long ago in Northern Africa. That territory was lush and fertile at the time of the Roman Empire. Large areas were cleared and cultivated to provide food for the Empire. With the land exposed to the tropical sun and wind, much of the fertile soil blew away and the Sahara Desert grew. There is some evidence that enough of the soil ended up in the Mediterranean Sea that the harbours of some large trading centers were silted up and became unusable.

Expanding populations also threaten forests. In some countries there is no land available for poor people to grow their food unless they clear remaining forest lands. Wood is also needed for cooking in many places. Without appropriate reforestation programs, people have to go further and further to find supplies. In some places the wood is so limited that people have turned to using animal dung and crop residues to cook their food, depriving the soil of much-needed nutrients.

Ground Water Depletion

Although water is a renewable resource, it is not always available in the quantities desired. There are numerous dry lands where rainfall and surface water are being supplemented with well water from underground reservoirs.

In dry areas, such underground reserves are often remnants of bygone days when more rain fell in the territory. In other cases, they represent the accumulation of small amounts of rainfall that soaked into the ground year after year for hundreds and thousands of years.

These sources of water grow fine crops, especially considering the abundance of sunlight in many dry areas, but when ground water is used at a rate far faster than the rate of accumulation, these reservoirs can be depleted. In the U.S. mid-west, wells which used to produce water at 50 feet are now going dry at 200 feet. A similar situation threatens agricultural efforts in the Middle East.

Non-Renewable Resource Depletion

Non-renewable resources are resources that occur on Earth in finite quantities. These are of two sorts: those that can be reused and those that are consumed in use. Reusable resources like metals and nutrient materials can be managed, to provide us with an ever-present inventory of materials to cycle continuously in our service. Use of these resources should include in their pricing the cost of returning them to where they are available to be used again.

The fuel resources — coal, oil and gas — are a different matter. When they are burned, they are gone. The enormous quantities that we inherited from the previous billion years of life on Earth have been tapped to the point that they will no longer be considered abundant within a lifetime. The fossil fuel reserves can be likened to the yolk of an egg — a supply of energy that enables a young creature to grow strong enough to live on its own when the inherited reserve is gone. When we have used up our yolk of fossil fuel resources, will we have built a society that can live without them?

Energy Depletion

There are two ways to deal with the problem of energy shortages. One is to develop new sources of energy; the other is to find ways to make the energy we have go further. During the "energy crisis" of the early 1970's, both conservation and exploration were undertaken on a vast scale. Looking back, it has been calculated that the amount of energy saved since that time, through conservation measures, is greater than the amount of energy that was discovered over the same period.

In the case of Brazil it has been calculated that $4 billion spent on energy-efficient motors, light bulbs, water heaters and other appliances would save the need to build $16 billion worth of generation capacity. Similar calculations for the United States indicate that the entire national debt could be paid off in a decade or two with the money saved through energy conservation. Although enormous amounts of energy can be saved, there is the problem of how to pay for the energy efficient appliances in the first place. Building new power plants is an established practice. Power companies are accustomed to raising money for mega-projects and banks are only too happy to collect the interest on the large amounts of money involved. In the end, due to the finite reality of energy reserves, we would come out ahead by conserving.

Loss of Habitat and Species Extinction

As forests and wetlands are destroyed to make way for development of one sort or another, the plants and animals

129

that inhabit those areas have to find other places to live or perish for want of a suitable home. In an increasing number of places, this loss of habitat is leading to the extinction of species. Estimates suggest that as many as 2,000 species are being lost each year. Even the tremendous wave of extinctions that wiped out the dinosaurs was minor in comparison to the speed of species loss in the twentieth century.

As members of the planetary community, all living things have a right to survival. Each time a species is lost, the whole world is poorer.

If one fails to make the moral connections of the right to existence or the aesthetics of a bountiful Earth, there are concerns centered on human interests as well:

• All life forms are interconnected. The more species that we crowd out of existence, the weaker the web of life that supports us all.

• There is also the question of genetic resources. Many problems with our food crops have been solved by finding wild plant species to interbreed with our seed stock to produce hardy, resistant strains.

• All of our food crops and domestic animals came originally from the wild. The abundance of life forms in tropical forests and elsewhere still holds the potential of additional species that could contribute to our food needs.

• Similarly, many of the medical drugs that we use have been derived from wild plants. If we lose the source of new materials, we could find our planet lacking in genetic resources when we need them.

Genetic Monopolies

Even among our established food plants, there is a threat to the availability of genetic resources. As a result of extensive specialized plant breeding and the expansion of biological engineering, there are numerous varieties of new plants on the market. These new seeds are often produced as economic investments, and lobbying by seed companies has resulted in laws allowing seed varieties to be patented.

In addition to owning sole rights to sell specific life forms, the large seed companies have also been buying up smaller seed companies and discontinuing their lines, so as to increase their own share of the market. This has resulted in the loss of many plant varieties. For example, 85 percent of the apple varieties that grew in North America a century ago no longer exist. Not only is genetic diversity being reduced, but the varieties being lost are often ones that can be maintained by individuals and communities without access to complex technology. There are heritage seed groups trying to preserve traditional varieties which could use help from any experienced gardeners that are interested. In Canada, write to the Heritage Seed Program, RR#3 Uxbridge, Ontario, L9P 1R3.

Poverty

Poverty is both a major cause and effect of environmental problems. The United Nations' World Commission on Environment and Development advises that if the destruction of the world's environment is to be averted, poverty must be overcome.

The Third World has lost the global Monopoly game. The rich get richer and the poor get poorer. Rather than collectively packing up the game and playing something else, we are condemning hundreds of millions of people to scratch a living out of their already stressed surroundings. In desperation people will do whatever they can to stay alive. Forests disappear and deserts advance. This pattern aggravates climatic changes and spawns political instability, affecting the rich as well as the poor. Yet, the game goes on. In 1987, the net flow of resources between the rich and poor countries was around $35 billion in favor of the rich. By 1992, this figure had risen to around $50 billion.

Huge amounts of money have been loaned to Third World countries to pursue development schemes and to purchase armaments. Often, much of the money returned directly to the lending countries, as their engineering firms and weapons manufacturers got the contracts from the borrowers. Many development projects have been used to produce crops and raw materials for export. The last decade has seen markets flooded with such commodities from the many developing nations. As a result, prices have fallen dramatically, leaving many exporters unable even to pay the interest on their loans. Having to borrow more money, just to make interest payments, forces the debtors to try and expand production for export, further stressing their soils and forests and shattering their hopes of rising out of poverty. The developed world, on the other hand, benefits both from collecting interest payments and from lower commodity prices.

Clearly, the population explosion in the Third World complicates their plight. Studies show that education and economic security are major influences on the decline of population growth rates. In a poor country with no form of social security, children are the only insurance against misery in old age. Furthermore, without clean water and other basic health facilities, many children die. Consequently, to protect against loss, it seems desirable to have many children.

If we stopped looking at the people of the developing world as a source of cheap resources and a market to be exploited, and let them focus on providing for their own needs, they could quickly improve their lots. Local demand for agricultural produce and basic manufactured goods would stimulate their economies, if they weren't so preoccupied with trying to raise foreign exchange to pay interest on the rich world's money collection. (It is interesting to note that much of this "money collection" had its origin in colonial times when resources and labour were taken outright from the same territories that now are crippled by debt.) The elimination of desperation in poor countries would relieve environmental stress, and the developing countries could make their own contributions to the global challenge of finding sustainable ways for humanity to exist on Earth. We cannot be successful in securing our future if they are forced to destroy the same planet on which we live.

Problems involved with both tolerance and resource supply

Destruction of Aboriginal Cultures

The effects of resources depletion are not being felt equally by all people. Cultures which have long traditions of living within particular territories face obliteration when the industrial world becomes covetous of the resources of their lands. The lives and cultures of aboriginal people are so intertwined with the land and life around them that to move them is often to destroy them.

Dam building is one of the greatest culprits in dislocating peoples from their home territories. Thousands of acres of prime land are being flooded by large hydro reservoirs. Clearing the rain forest areas for agriculture is another offender, as it requires the displacement of traditional peoples and their ways of life. In both these cases, the developers of such grand designs often lose interest in relocating displaced people once they are out of the way. Many such schemes have been short-lived due to the silting up of reservoirs or the inappropriateness of the land for growing anything but forest.

Again, if our recognition of the right to life and to justice are not strong enough to allow people their traditional ways, we would do well to consider the knowledge that aboriginal peoples have gathered over time about how to live from their homelands. Often, they inhabit marginal areas and have done so for centuries without upsetting the balance of nature. When we see modern technology destroying such places, often in less than a generation, we should ask: What do these people know that we don't? There is much to be gained from their answers.

Militarism

An inventory of environmental problems wouldn't be complete without a mention of militarism. Militarism is both a serious polluter and a strain on resource supplies.

In the aftermath of wars, there is often much territory that has lost its productive potential due to bomb craters, unexploded shells in the soil, land mines and areas that were intentionally defoliated or fire-bombed to expose troop movements or cause economic disruption.

Nuclear weapons offer the possibility of total ecological disruption. One percent of the nuclear arsenal could bring on nuclear winter. Great upward moving currents of air caused by nuclear explosions would throw huge quantities of dust, ashes and smoke up into the atmosphere. In addition to spreading nuclear radiation over the entire globe, it would block the sun's light and winter would be world-wide for some years.

A perspective on the misallocation of resources can be found in Ruth Sivard's book *World Military and Social Expenditure*. This detailed collection of statistics is illustrated at one point with a list of what could be funded with 5 percent of the money spent on arms. The list includes:

• Safe water and sanitation facilities for the third of the world's population who do not have them.

• Food supplements for the World's 900,000,000 malnourished children.

• Community health centers for the 1 billion people without such services.

• Prenatal care and family planning education.

• Immunization for all children.

• Environmental clean-up of nuclear bomb plants.

• And a number of other much-needed Health Care and Education related services.

It is noteworthy that, of the huge reserves of oil on the Alaskan North coast, one half is reserved for the US military.

Another major concern is that a significant portion of the world's technical creativity is committed to military work and contributes little to overcoming non-military threats to our security.

Over-Population

Whatever the effects of human activity on the Earth, they are further aggravated by each additional individual adding his or her consumption and waste to the global situation. Yet, for some reason, over-population is often denied as an issue.

Some say it is not a problem of population so much as it is a problem of distribution. After all, one person born in North American will use twenty to forty times as many resources and produce twenty to forty times as much waste as a person born in India. No doubt the lot of the world's poor would improve immensely, and environmental problems with them, if global equity were an established practice. But even if equity were achieved, would we not again be stressing the planet when our population is double that of today? And what of the next doubling after that?

History shows that human beings have repeatedly adapted their way of living to accommodate expanding numbers. Our current five-and-a-half billion is able to survive only because of a number of non-sustainable practices. Maybe with an appropriate reorganization of techniques and priorities, we can support our current numbers in a sustainable way. Maybe we can't.

It doesn't take complex mathematics to figure out that sooner or later an ever-expanding population will come to grief. In nature, such population explosions typically end with an 80 to 90 percent die-off, as the environment finally collapses under the stress.

It is ironic that the compassion and dedicated work that have led to lower infant mortality and longer lives are leading to unprecedented suffering, for want of equally effective control over births.

We have done a remarkable job at keeping up with the expanding population. If we could provide old age security that didn't depend on having many children; basic medical services that assure that the children who are born will live; and the knowledge needed to plan families, populations would stabilize. Without having to double the production of food and shelter over the next twenty years, we would very quickly catch up with human need. Once we catch up, it will be easy to provide those services that would lead to a stable population. Once again the question: where will the money come from to solve the problems that, once solved, would free up more than enough money to solve those problems?

* * *

All the issues detailed here require us to become aware of the effects our ways of life have on the planet. We have to educate ourselves to make these connections and learn to act on the considerations that arise from them, just as we act on the conditions arising from the seasons, the weather and our economic circumstances. Our ability to act on global considerations, or our inability to do so, will be the factor that decides humanity's fate on Earth.

Epilogue

Transformation

If you've just finished the last 32-pages of bad news, you probably need some cheering up. It's true, we face perilous and complex problems and it is important not to underestimate the danger we are in.

With that caution noted, we can set our sights on the day when environmental imbalance will be a curiosity discussed in text books. Our times will be noted in historical terms as the turbulent passage of civilization from adolescence to maturity. I bet my life we will rise to the challenge.

Never has a creature been so well-suited to survive. Our ability to sense the world is unparalleled. Our eyes, ears and other senses, although not the best, are nevertheless very functional. When coupled with our telescopes, microscopes, radar, sonar, satellites, submarines and other such tools, we are orders of magnitude more perceptive than any creature that has ever lived. Our ability to recognize patterns in the information we gather is enormous and we have a great capacity to remember. We remember not just as individuals, but as a culture, through traditions, literature and libraries which span generations. Add to this our ability to communicate across the room and around the globe and we can see a truly remarkable species, a prime candidate for survival. With our talents and adaptability, people could very well enjoy life on Earth millions of years from now.

How much trauma will we have to go through before we catch our balance within the planetary ecosystem? The answer depends on how long it takes for our societies to recognize, admit to and act upon the responsibilities that come with being a mature species. Our lives must be maintained in a sustainable fashion through respect for the land, other life, other people and by learning to enjoy the wonders of being alive.

Sustainability is the key. People are quick to recognize the nature of the obligation, but many are not ready to admit that it is time to grow up. They pretend they haven't heard.

The Guideposts are a drum beat calling for sustainability. There are other beats making the same call. Around the world wherever well-meaning people hear the beat they are joining in. The sound is getting louder. Listen carefully and you will hear it again and again from one sector after another. Choose your instrument and join the call. Beat out the sound for the love of life. Beat it for clean air and pure water. Beat it for the forests, fields and living things. Beat it for wholesome food. Beat it for the children. Beat it for yourself. When the sound rings out so loud and clear that no one can ignore it, the priority of sustainability will be declared, not just from the lips but from the heart. The world of our dreams will appear possible, first in our minds and then in the product of our work. Excitement and anticipation will mount as we realize that the extraordinary ability of humankind is finally being applied to take responsibility for our presence on Earth. It will be cause for celebration.

A transformation of civilization will be witnessed much like that which a caterpillar undergoes when it becomes a butterfly. Within its cocoon, every cell of the caterpillar takes on the task of rearranging its own physical substance, of preparing itself for the form it will assume when the transformation is complete. Some systems, like the nervous system, maintain their functions, but they too adapt to accommodate the new form. When every part has attended to the work at hand, the butterfly emerges.

Widespread enthusiasm for sustainability would be our cocoon. With the direction clarified, each of us knows our own life best and has the best qualifications to start rearranging our affairs for the butterfly we must become. Within the consensus, business, government and other institutions would adapt or be adapted to the requirements of sustainability. Personal changes will reinforce institutional change and institutional changes will make it easier to live sustainably. When our butterfly emerges, humankind will have come of age.

Materials Available from:

Guideposts for a Sustainable Future
P.O. Box 374, Merrickville, Ontario,
Canada, K0G 1N0

The materials listed below can help spread the basic reference for sustainability, clarify what it means and focus debate on the kind of future we want to build.

Video: *Guideposts for a Sustainable Future*:

This 23 minute production makes it easy to share the message of *Planning for Seven Generations* with family, friends and others. Included with the cassette is a booklet outlining a discussion which greatly enhances viewing. The video follows the progression of ideas in chapter 3 of this book. Page 14 briefly outlines the suggested discussion. $25.00*

Book: *Planning for Seven Generations:*

For an additional copy of this book $4.95
For wholesale orders, (five or more) subtract 40% per book.

Book: *Change the World I Want to Stay On:*

Also by Mike Nickerson. Published in 1977, this environmental classic was called:
"one of the most important books of the decade"
                    Natural Life Magazine.
                                    $7.75